Jon & Jenni,
What a blessing
having met
you in [...]
God drew
his [...] to yr
Lov to all.
Susan Lemon

Our Conversations with God

Life in the Spirit

Susan Lemon

xulon PRESS

To My Husband, David

Thank you for helping me to see this project through.
Thank you for being willing to do whatever it takes to hold the
Lord's hand.
You are a man of courage!
I love you.

ACKNOWLEDGEMENTS

With special thanks:

TO my husband, David, for your love, understanding, patience and most of all your loyalty to God.

TO my girls, Danielle and Alex, for giving up some "mommy time" so this book could be written and of course sharing the computer.

TO John David and Deanna Stewart, for being there when we've needed you and for being some of the most heartfelt, trustworthy and true prayer partners we've known.

TO the Pastoral Staff of Parkview Baptist Church, for not forgetting us when we moved to Tennessee and for your continued love and prayers.

TO Nita Tin and Susie Westbrook, for the proofreading of this book and your love for seeing this project through.

TO my mother in-law, Ruth Lemon, who encouraged, inspired and pushed me to finish God's work regardless of the cost.

TO C.T. Cozart and the Red Bank Baptist Church Family, first and foremost for your love for the Lord, your warmth and concern and your willingness to open your arms wide to our family.

TO my Chattanooga buddies, Brad and Michelle Shepard, Eadress Baxter, Jina Kimball, Sharon Lawson, and Ginger Haymaker whose prayers, faithful friendships, relentless prayer sessions and endless study of God's word have encouraged me to be all that God wants me to be. You have truly been the "light" when our days were dim and have stood behind us regardless. You are eternal friends!

TO Diann Sivley, Jill Noll and Pam Klapp, for your devotion to studying God's word and for your lessons of love during each Bible Study and for your arms that embraced me when it was difficult to stand tall.

TO my parents, Benny and Bootsie Morgan, for being willing to let go so we could move so many hundreds of miles away from home. I love you.

*"Faith is the sweet scent blowing softly
in the winds of heaven."*

Susan Lemon

CONTENTS

PROLOGUE

Many inspired, meaningful writers start out writing with a specific idea, plan, or some purpose in mind. Those are truly gifted writers. I, however, did not begin writing this book that way. In fact I had no plan of writing this book at all, but the stories formed patterns and the patterns turned into chapters and the chapters formed the book you hold in your hands today. By the leading of the Holy Spirit, this book has been formed together by no ingenuity of my own. I am not capable of such. I am certain, however, that through the ease of which this book was written that there were supernatural words that seem to flow with little effort. I am neither a theologian nor a biblical scholar; I am an ordinary person that writes not from her own self, but from a Higher Source. The words are by no means my own to claim. I hope to show you that by the leading of the Lord in my life, this creation, this book, is an example of how God uses every single experience, trauma or circumstance in our lives for His glory.

Let me also say that God allowed me to get to know Him intimately through my personal relationship with Jesus Christ, which is the basis of this entire book- obtaining and maintain a deeply, personal relationship with our Lord and Savior, Jesus, despite fear, frustration and many other uncertainties that have existed in my life. Walk with me for a moment through a glance of how to get started if you are unsure about your relationship with the Lord or unsure about where God wants you to be, or just unsure about your future.

Where am I?

There is nothing more unsettling than being lost. It's alarming. It's frightening. It doesn't bring us peace. Being lost separates us from where we are going, and quite often we don't want to admit we are lost. We just wander around in hopes that we will find our way eventually. Being lost out on the freeway and living a life separate and apart from God may produce the same feelings, but the outcome is tragically different. The only way we can keep from wasting our lives and being lost is through God alone. God is life. He alone sustains our lives, our every breath we take and gives us our every heartbeat. God gave His son, Jesus, so we could live and live and live. Without having Jesus as Lord and Savior over our lives we cannot live. And certainly we cannot live the life described below which is one of the most intriguing subjects that exists today – heaven.

Picture yourself looking up at the bluest sky your eyes have ever seen. The grass is the finest shade of green that exists. The very dirt of the earth calls out to you to reach down and feel its pure texture as you reach down to run it through your hands. Your eyes cannot take in all of the massive colors that explode across the land as you look out over the field. You arise and begin walking and you see water in the distance, but it's not ordinary water, it is water that is so pure and clean that is glimmers as pure gold as it moves back and forth dancing to the Lord's command. The sunlight is so consuming that you want to lean your face upward into the pure beams of light that are radiating out and just soak up as much of God's love as you possibly can. You cannot remove yourself from this place. You have arrived at your final destination. It is heaven. Your faith has saved you. You think back to when you called out the name of Jesus so long ago and prayed a simple prayer asking God to save you from your sins. You are seeing the results of your prayer and your belief in God. Your call was not because you saw God but because you believed by faith. Your faith has placed you here. Heaven is no longer a mystery; a thought, a dream, a story or some far away place. It is here. You see it with your very own eyes. It is truly Heaven.

As you begin walking across the land you see all of these people that are truly rejoicing, praising God and giving thanks to the Father, and you feel such an intense desire to join them that your feet cannot be contained, your voice cannot do anything but give praise to God. Your entire body is free. Free to love. Free to care. Free to give God all of the glory. You look around and you see so many people that you feel are family but you've never met them before. There is a strange sense of being intimately connected to all of those around you. There is peacefulness about those you are rejoicing with. You realize again it is truly heaven.

As you make your way down the path, through the fields and over the massive hills and peaks, you walk as if you are walking with a purpose. You know exactly where you are going but you've never been there before. It's as if your every dream, every desire is coming true. You cannot explain the feeling of such contentment that is present. You have never felt this type of contentment before or this type of massive joy that is bursting out of your entire body. You begin running as your feet cannot walk any longer. You run and run, but you never tire. You realize again it is truly heaven.

As we take a glimpse into heaven and what our lives will be like for all of eternity, we know that God is true. God is real, and God is so giving. God gave us His Son, His scriptures, and His very breath to give us a glimpse of what our heavenly home will be like. *You alone are Lord. You made the heavens, even the highest heavens, and all their starry host, the earth and all that is on it, the seas and all that is in them. You give life to everything, and the multitudes of heaven worship you. Nehemiah 9:6.* As truly magnificent as heaven is, the reality is that if you have not accepted Jesus Christ as your Lord and Savior today, the most important conversation you will ever need to have with God goes something like this,

Lord,

I confess I am a sinner. I believe that Jesus died on the cross for my sins, and I want you to come into my life and change me. I want to be saved. Please come into my heart and change my ways, help me to begin a new life with you and help me to follow you with all of my heart. In Jesus name I pray, Amen.

It is by faith alone that you are saved. God's word tells us *that if you confess with your mouth, "Jesus is Lord," and believe in your heart that God raised him from the dead, you will be saved. For it is with your heart that you believe and are justified, and it is with your mouth that you confess and are saved. Romans 10:9-10.*

As the feelings of uncertainty about eternity and your life pass from old to new, you are now assured of your eternal place in heaven with the King. It is your gift from God this very day. Pass it along and take the second step of your journey, a life filled with Christ.

As you journey along and begin reading this book, you will see each story for what they are – real. Some are my own experiences and some of the stories are based on persons that I've met, encountered and divinely entered into conversation with through the workings of our Lord and Savior. But rest assured that the stories are true, the people are real and the massive amounts of transformation in my life due to those experiences and in some cases, trauma, have added meaning, dimension and a firm foundation from which I stand. Some of the people God placed in my life have helped to turn my face upward and have shaped and formed who I am today- a redeemed child of God. I pray you will be blessed as you turn each page and begin your own *Conversations with God.*

Our Conversations with God

Introduction

INTRODUCTION

As my husband and I began our spiritual journey we walked through some of the most outlandish of times! God is full of surprises. God spoke deep, meaningful and insightful themes into our journey that has taken us from living a scarcely Christian existence to a life extreme with Christ.

Our conversations with God are real; they are full of God's love and compassion, and they have oftentimes begun simply and ended in ways that are so unthinkable and immeasurable with human eyes. Our journey began with one simple prayer, a huge answer and times of holding on for our lives. That was the faith trip.

Our journey continued with God, and our conversations deepened in meaning and became our every breath, as we held on to each of God's words and His unfailing promises to trust Him and Him alone. On that trip we spent everything right down to the last coin! And then God asked us to trust some more. We did, and we found ourselves loving God more for the unusual predicaments He placed us in.

As time went on we spent great efforts trying to learn the heart of the Lord. He picked us up and let us meet a variety of people. Some of those meetings are etched deeply in our hearts today as a token of God's love and affection for us, His children. And some of which we have yet to experience. We are still on that part of the journey, and my prayer is that part will never end.

Drawing nearer to God in the midst of pain, suffering and struggles began the next part of our walk with God. God chose to walk in our lives boldly at the oddest of times and in the direst of circumstances that often left us in awe of how massive His hand of transformation really is. He visited us for many conversations in the process of refining our innermost thoughts to become one with Him. All of this left us strengthened, enlightened, motivated, and captured by the very hand of Christ.

At any given time, day or night, my husband and I shared our thoughts, our feelings, and our love with the Lord; we call that part of the journey simply prayer. Our prayer journey brought us face to face with life and death situations and took us down many roads not yet discovered by most. Some of those conversations with God were by far some of the most intriguing words spoken by persons desperate for God to answer them. That part of the journey motivated us and still motivates us to this very day to simply pray.

As we pressed onward, we found we needed more knowledge about God. We got it quickly in God's Holy Word. Our many, many conversations with God asking Him to breathe His insight and His divine wisdom about His scriptures into us brought us face to face with the enemy as never before. As we learned more, we were trampled on more but God picked us up and dusted us off and set our feet on firm ground rooted in His Holy Word. The lessons learned from that part of the journey literally saved us from falling away from God in the midst of the fiercest trials we faced and set our lives and our marriage firmly in His care.

The sweetest part of our journey was walking hand-in-hand with our Lord and Savior Himself in developing a marriage that was and is today deeply committed to Christ first, our love for each other second, and, of course lots and lots of chocolate pudding. Sweet success and lots of love brought us to walk along a path we never thought we would experience with the Lord- our sex life. God reached out and put our marriage under construction for a period and then firmly gathered our hands together and taught us about sex, marriage and God. Priceless! As we learned that God's hand of delivering power was sure, swift, and real, we rested for a while.

As we rested, we found that we needed nothing more than to rest merely in God himself. We took long breaks from stress-filled lives and took slow, leisurely walks basking in God's glory, His promises, and His ever-changing plan for our lives. We melted our hearts to God's plan and had many conversations with God simply praising Him for the very places He took us to. And as we continued to journey along, we saw no other place for our lives except in the Hand of the Father. We nestled in closely and bathed ourselves in His sheer luxury, the presence of the Most Holy One, the King of kings, Lord of lords, and the true Prince of Peace. That brought us to where we are today in God's Holy arms of love and care, desperately seeking a continued life filled by only the hands of Christ!

Our Conversations with God

On Faith & Obedience

Chapter 1

The Ultimate Interruption

The ride was serene as we made our way to what we thought was just a weekend get-a-way. My husband and I had renewed our love for the Lord and each other and we decided to go and celebrate what God had done in our lives. The reservations were made, the kids were taken care of and we spent a long weekend of togetherness, spiritual renewal and a time of new beginnings. Little did we know it would be the ultimate ride with God hovering closely at our sides.

As we made our way to the hotel we took in all of the sites and the scenery and anticipated a weekend without any interruptions. We enjoyed our time alone as we talked about our children, our lives and our future. Late one Sunday afternoon my husband and I joined hands as we sat on the bed in the hotel room and went to the Lord in prayer. Our conversation with God went something like this,

Lord, you are so mighty! Your works amaze us. We sit here today because of you. You are our Savior, our Redeemer, and our guiding force. Show us your love today. Show us your love, Father...........

As we continued to pray, we eventually walked away from that prayer time uplifted, encouraged, bewildered, and amazed, as we knew that God was getting ready to move us and move us big time! The Lord began to quietly reveal to us the massive plans of change He had for our future. We had no idea this interruption was coming! But God did. And He waited for us to respond.

We could have walked away from that prayer time with uncertainty, doubt, and fear but instead we had a sure peace that even though our lives were getting ready to change, holding the hands of God Himself during that change would be better than any futuristic plan we could have ever made on our own.

If God had walked in at that very moment and said, "I want you to quit your job, sell your new home, leave your family and friends, uproot your children and move to a land you've never seen before and begin a new life there in service to me," we may have rushed to the elevator trying to get out! But God in His sovereignty and His compassion for His children only revealed to us what we needed to know at that exact time. We knew we were moving away. We didn't know when or how but we knew we would be moving.

How would we begin to orchestrate a move of this magnitude that was ahead of us? We couldn't! God interrupted our day, our weekend and ultimately our future, and He had all of the answers we could possible need. God has the answer to every powerful question we can throw His way. His answers come when His divine time arrives. Our time had arrived and this interruption was certainly divine. God's plan for both David and me was to quit our jobs and give up our careers, sell our home, leave comfort and all we knew to be security behind.

As we contemplated how we would accomplish disconnecting from our homeland, we realized that we couldn't do that in our own strength. God would have to intervene. We became dependent on such a loving and Masterful God for every breath we were taking, and we knew that tiny prayers reap big answers, willing hands produce an abundance and that God uses even the smallest of His servants!

Comfortable as we were, nested in our Southern Louisiana home with our girls, we were just minutes away from family, friends, work, school and our church home. The Lord interrupted our plans and began working to unfold a masterful schedule of events in our lives. Intricately woven into God's plan was our friendship with John David and Deanna Stewart.

God so delicately placed this couple in our lives right before He began a mighty work of change and reconstruction. We didn't know why God was calling us to move away at the time and our future was very uncertain. We found it difficult to think of uprooting our children from their home and security, and we found no way to plan for our financial future or the many emotional needs that were surfacing daily. Our time spent with John David and Deanna brought new prayer partners for us, huge prayers, and an intimate view of a truly loving God who wants nothing more for us than His very best. It brought about a measure of faith that enabled us to move forward despite the many unanswered questions about our future. *Now faith is being sure of what we hope for and certain of what we do not see. Hebrews 11:1.* The everlasting arms of the Lord Jesus were present and provided comfort, assurance, hope, and promises of a future serving Him. *Cast your cares on the Lord and he will sustain you; he will never let the righteous fall. Psalm 55:22.* Taking firm hold of God's plan during that time provided the faith we needed to trust Him for all of our needs and a future filled with so much hope. Faith and action send a message to God – I believe and I'll prove it!

It simply didn't make sense for both of us to give up our jobs, but the Lord's plan was set, and we were to follow it and not look back. That was a big one. God was bigger! As we both gave up our only source of income, we didn't know how we would survive financially, but the Lord gave us peace. Faith is funny that way; it loves the unexpected. It simply thrives on God's unexpected gifts. Just weeks later my husband received cash proceeds from the sale of some property that had been literally unavailable for years. That was a God thing! We trusted, and He proved Himself faithful.

As we packed up for our journey, we found that faith meant putting one foot in front of the other when we couldn't see where we were walking. Faith also called for us to form our own parade when the world had deaf ears and blind eyes to the leading of the Lord in our lives, and we most definitely knew that faith began with God and would end with God; the middle was up to us! As we were swept away by God's care and God's plan for our lives, we embraced the whirlwind of change with every bit of energy we had. That was the obedience part of the journey and as for the interruption, it was simply the ultimate!

Chapter 2

God's Roadmap

What is God's best for us? Why is it that oftentimes God's best doesn't feel like our very best or what we would define as good for us? Why is that gap so defining and what can we do as children of the beloved in Christ do to fill that gap? For my family and me that gap became very apparent and widened with each turn we took. Eventually those widened gaps turned into small, tiny crevasses that ultimately defined our faith, reinforced our trust in God, and brought us into spacious lands abounding with all of God's love, care, and provisions.

As our journey began, my husband and I realized that God's very best for us was actually a call to have more of God, a higher standard, a greater place than where we were when we started. God simply wanted more for us! It was with that call that we often times felt uncertain, anxious, and unsure about our future. Those pressing feelings of uncertainty produced a gap that kept us from receiving God fully. God so desperately wants us to have more of Him that He oftentimes uses that gap to edge us in closely and wrap His arms around us, ultimately bringing unexpected, hidden treasures along the way and a walk with Him that can only be traced to His hand. As we began to trace the Father's hand in our lives, we went to Him in prayer. Our conversation with God went something like this,

Father, how we long to hear from you and know our purpose. Give us clarity, direction and vision. Let us hear from you. Allow our ears to be full of your purpose and not our own. Let our hearts be opened softly to your will. Help us to see clearly where you are leading us and every detail we need to know at this very second. We feel your hand in our lives making our path but we cannot see any further than that. Let there be light. Let there be clear vision. Let there be a clear path, a roadmap, that takes us only to the place you desire us to be. Give us confidence, confirmation, and most of all, your love, Father, your sweet, sweet love!

As we turned to our Heavenly Father in prayer, we felt such a love for the quietness of the moment and a tremendous desire to know exactly where we would be going and why we were going there. As it turned out, I believe we were actually praying for God's roadmap to breathe life into our journey and pep into our step. I'm convinced that God doesn't set out to keep secrets from His children or remain a mystery in our lives. A loving God who takes the hand of His child to instruct, guide, correct, provide, and to carry them along the path chosen not by man but by God, that is the Father.

The Lord said to Abram, "Leave your country, your people, and your father's household and go to the land that I will show you." Genesis 12:1. When God called Abram to go, it wasn't a warm feeling that he had nor was it a hunch; it was the voice of the Lord clearly speaking to His servant directing him on the path to take for the future in order to fulfill God's divine will in his life. When the Lord called Samuel, he didn't recognize the voice of the Lord but soon found out that, yes, God speaks to His children. *The Lord called Samuel a third time, and Samuel got up and went to Eli and said, "Here I am; you called me." Then Eli realized that the Lord was calling the boy. So Eli told Samuel, "Go and lie down, and if he calls you say, "Speak, Lord, for your servant is listening." So Samuel went and lay down in his place. The Lord came to Samuel and stood there, calling as at the other times, "Samuel! Samuel!" Then Samuel said, "Speak for your servant is listening." 1 Samuel 3:8-10.*

Discerning God's voice cannot come from our own ability, it is the power of the Lord that allows us to clearly hear His voice and follow His ways for our lives. Hearing the voice of the Lord is a mystery to most but a certainty to His children. I'm convinced of that. The voice of the Lord is certain. It is powerful. It is delicate and commanding all in the same breath. It can take an ordinary person and transform him into a vessel of trust and obedience regardless of the price to be paid. After all, God alone is the only one that truly knows what is ahead for you and for me.

God doesn't always call His people to uproot, but God does have a plan uniquely for each one of us. For us we felt the Spirit of the Lord in our lives firmly as He prepared us for our roadmap that was designed especially for our situation, our future, and us. God's roadmap only required two things of us - faith and obedience. *The Spirit of the Lord will rest on him- the spirit of wisdom and under-standing, the Spirit of counsel and of power, the Spirit of knowledge and of the fear of the Lord, Isaiah 11: 2.*

God's roadmap included bridges of waiting, a few collisions with the enemy, and some of the richest blessings we have ever received. And what we didn't know is that when God gives you a road map for your life, He also wants to give you gas money to get there! God directed our family to pick up and move and follow His roadmap wherever the destination might have been. God with His arms of love and goodness set our destination for Chattanooga, Tennessee. We didn't have jobs there nor did we have any family there. We didn't know anything about Chattanooga or the area, but God did. God had already gone ahead of us and prepared the path. And He stood anxiously with His mighty arms of love stretched out wide awaiting our arrival. But the enemy was camped out and wanted nothing more than for God's roadmap for our future to be doubted, feared and ultimately not followed. When moments of doubt crept in about our future, fear also crept in. Fear can keep us from all that God has for us. And oftentimes fear is so powerful that it takes God's divine power to remove it. Our conversation with God went something like this,

Lord, we are in need of you! Please remove this spirit of fear and

anxiety and replace it with a spirit of peace. We cannot survive without peace, for what you have called us to do. We know that you did not give us a spirit of timidity, but a spirit of power, of love, and of self-discipline. II Timothy 1:7. We trust you Lord. We will not be overcome by the enemy, and we will follow your plan; just give us peace in Jesus name.

God's feet of compassion swiftly came to our rescue, and He provided us with a sure spirit of peace instantly! The power of prayer unlocked God's power to push us forward, give us rest and bring calming relief. Following God's roadmap meant talking to the driver frequently, and we did that in prayer!

The next few months would prove God's power is massive and that He alone is God! Events in our move did not unfold as we had thought they would in a smooth pattern of going from point A to point B. It just didn't happen that way. There were challenges with obtaining a home. Ultimately, God stepped in and provided a temporary solution. But even after that major obstacle was no longer an issue, there were still more bumps in the road.

We were three days away from the movers coming to pick up our furniture and still had not finalized our paperwork. God was still in control, but Satan was hard at work. The movers arrived on that rainy Thursday ready to go. When they asked my husband for confirmation on the "new home address" we both just looked at each other and grinned. We knew we didn't have another home address to give the man. My husband just told the movers to head up towards Chattanooga, and we would buzz them on the cell phone with an address as soon as we were sure. I thought, how could we not know where we were moving to? How could this have happened? Why didn't God allow us to sign papers on the new home and leave no uncertainty that we would have a place to live? Why?

When those questions began to run through our minds, our very close friend and Pastor, Merlin Liverman had prayer with us many times and was so comforting when he softly offered his words of wisdom. Brother Merlin had this way of communicating God's message to us softly and honestly. He didn't paint a rosy picture nor did he give us a sense of false hope. He spoke God's truth plainly and clearly. His example was vivid, thought provoking, and so full of God's power. It was about the needs of Moses, great as they were. Brother Merlin explained that God didn't part the Red Sea two weeks in advance for Moses and that God divinely waited until Moses was right there at the bank to perform that miracle. How true! I believe that in our minds we were expecting every single detail of our move to fall into this great vacuum of smoothness, never to have to rely on God to work out the bumps. That simply wasn't God's plan!

We regained a sure and certain peace as we began our ten-hour drive to our new home; we had many, many conversations with God, one of which went something like this,

Lord, we are getting real close to the shore. Our toes are in the water. We need that sea parted!

We pressed forward, continued driving and yes rested in the Lord. We had an overwhelming feeling of God's presence with us and only had just one more hurdle to cross. In the very deepest of our hearts we felt God speak to us, and His conversation with us went something like this,

My Children, you will see yet another miracle performed between now and the time you settle in. Know that I am God and rest in me.

Well, this news was great, we thought, but what we didn't know was that this test would push us farther than the last! We traveled to our new home with our funds in the form of a cashier's check. We made our way to the bank to open a new account once we got to Chattanooga, and we soon found out that our cashier's check wouldn't be honored until it was held for three days! It was a Monday morning about 10am, and we were scheduled to sign papers at 4pm that day, and our furniture was being delivered on Tuesday. At that specific moment we had a worthless cashier's check. We were stunned! There wasn't enough time to drive or fly back to our old bank, which was about ten hours away, and get cash. As I hung my head in the face of a very sweet bank teller who was just following the rules, I thought, Lord, we are just hours from having our furniture dropped in a vacant parking lot and no home. My quiet conversation with God went something like this,

Lord, Lord, help us! We can't get to any funds right now. We have nowhere for our furniture to be delivered, and we don't know what to do. How in the world are you going to pull this one off? They aren't budging on the bank policy. I just don't understand. We do not have anywhere to turn but you!

After that conversation with God, I suddenly realized that God promised us that we would see another miracle, and this was clearly it! We left the bank and drove around in silence when our oldest daughter told us that she thought it would be a good idea to pull over and pray. God always prompts people to pray right before He works a miracle. This time He used my oldest daughter, Danielle, who was nine years old at the time to do just that - pray. Danielle didn't know of the circumstances, yet the Lord was using her. She led our prayer, and her conversation with God went something like this,

Lord, my Mom and Dad need you. Whatever they need, I know you can do. Amen.

How humbling her prayer was and how soothing her words were to our ears. We continued to run errands and nearly two hours later, the bank called and said our funds had come in through the wire and we could pick up our check! Pure miracle. Funds that were transferred by wire and not supposed to show up until midnight or later suddenly appeared within a few hours. We picked up our check at 2pm, and we were signing papers at 4pm that day, with only two hours to spare! God is true to His promises and that move would not have been possible in our own strength, ingenuity, or might. God moved mountains to see that we followed His roadmap, and it required a measure of faith I didn't know existed!

God spoke- He gave us courage to follow His directions. God intervened- He gave us provisions to follow Him. God blessed- He gave us more than we ever expected. God's roadmap didn't make any sense to us, but did Noah begin building the Ark based on common sense? I think not. Noah just accepted the assignment and went about his task, odd as it was. *By faith Noah, when warned about things not yet seen, in holy fear built an ark to save his family. By his faith he condemned the world and became heir of the righteousness that comes by faith. Hebrews 11:7.*

Faith and obedience are the two hands that meet together and are bound by God's voice that resounds loudly, clearly, and abundantly in the lives of his children. *For I know the plans I have for you, declares the Lord, plans to prosper you and not to harm you, plans to give you hope and a future. Jeremiah 29:11.* God's very best for us was wound up tightly in a twisting and winding road that ultimately proved to be not our roadmap but a roadmap that gave us more than we started with. It was God's best for us! And those gaps that were great and expansive at the very beginning of the journey dwindled down smaller and smaller until our faith was great enough to fill in even the tiniest of cracks that appeared. Our faith can fill the cracks of doubt and uncertainty in our lives when no other glue or adhesive comes close to getting the job done.

Trusting God and following His roadmap for us meant taking the road of oneness fast and furiously instead of the way we preferred, slowly and gingerly. It meant giving up the things we cherished most in life only for a loving God to pour out His very best, His most precious of blessings of sustenance on us! Sweet!

Chapter 3

Chocolate Dipped Choices

We spend a lifetime making choices. Choices, choices, choices! We do it each day without even realizing it. We decide what we are going to do for the day, we do it, and then when our plans go sour, we shake our heads in confusion or, worse yet, we shake our fists at God for allowing calamity or unexpected events to arise in our lives. Choices made independent of God may just be an invitation for turmoil, distress, and needless suffering in our lives. But making choices by the Father's will only brings about glory to Him! And peace is a certainty when our choices are made through prayerful times alone with the Father. *A wise son heeds his father's instruction. Proverbs 13:1a. For I have kept the ways of the Lord; I have not done evil by turning from my God. Psalm 18:21.*

Keeping the Lord's ways opens our vessel to live our lives according to the Father's plan, in the Spirit. *Those who live according to the sinful nature have their minds set on what that nature desires; but those who live in accordance with the Spirit have their minds set on what the Spirit desires. Romans 8:5.* That Spirit-filled vessel has an open heart, an open mind and allows God to mold and shape us to His divine will in each area of our lives. Yearning for the will of the Father, our choices are very different now. The choices we previously made, independent of God, now look very different, very plain. They are vanilla choices! But when we stop making choices in line with what we want and we begin seeking the Lord in prayer for what God wants in our lives, those are the chocolate dipped choices! Simply divine!

God in His tender arms of care and His quiet voice of guidance used my tiny, little daughter, who was three at the time to send me to the Father seeking direction in the oddest of circumstances. I'm convinced that God uses even the tiniest of His children to guide us in our decisions and set our feet to the Father's path. Our youngest daughter Alex and I made our way home from preschool one day, and she told me that she wanted to take gymnastics at another place where her friend was going. I dismissed the idea because she was already taking gymnastics at her preschool. God was at work trying to point me in the right direction, but I wasn't listening. A few weeks later Alex was invited to a birthday party at the very place she wanted to take Gymnastics at. As we were walking around the place, I began to feel the Lord moving and wondered if I should look into Alex taking gymnastics there. My conversation with the Lord went something like this,

Lord, I know you know the plans you have for us but this seems crazy to let Alex take gymnastics at two different places. Just show me your will and give me strength to follow it no matter what.

This gymnastics class ranked very high as being frivolous, a big time waster and totally unnecessary, but I felt the hand of the Lord pushing me to just do it, so I had a choice to make – chocolate or vanilla? I could have followed God's plan, which seemed odd and irrational, or followed my own plan, which seemed logical and the better choice. Life in the Spirit clearly yelled out to me, "Go God's way," so I did, odd as it was. I spoke to my husband and signed Alex up for another gymnastics class.

The first week we anxiously drove to the new gymnastics class with baited breath. My husband and I couldn't wait to see what God was going to do there. We watched, waited, watched some more and then that was it. The class was over. Nothing happened. Simply nothing. I was confused, perplexed and unsure about it all. My conversation with God went something like this,

Uh Lord, I simply don't understand.

Again I had a choice to make and God's way is always best! I continued taking her to gymnastics. Week two and week three went by and nothing happened at all. Nothing. We drove Alex to gymnastics and watched her class again and again. And then on week four God's plan began to unfold.

As I sat nestled into the couch all prepared to just read a while, I noticed this lady extending her loving hands over two children who had very unusual accents. That sparked my attention, so I asked the lady about the children. She said the children were Dutch and that English was their second language. She began telling me how she started taking care of the children while their parents got settled into their new home in the United States and that this temporary babysitting job turned into over a five-year assignment! Her love was so apparent for the small girl and the overjoyed, high-spirited little boy.

While sitting on the couch very comfy and cozy, I felt the Lord tugging on me to move aside and let the Holy Spirit begin working. I quietly prayed for guidance, and the words began to just flow out of me like a fountain spewing the sweetest of waters onto the most fertile of grounds. The woman, Idella, a very rooted, God-loving woman, had been praying for direction in her life because the children were clearly not babies anymore, and she was uncertain of what she needed to do when they entered school soon. Torn about this decision and desperately not wanting to leave the children, she had sought the Lord for weeks and weeks. As I sat on the couch next to Idella, words of love, encouragement, and comfort kept pouring out from me onto her as the Father gave me my words. Her eyes filled with tears of joy that anyone would even notice the love she had for these children. I reminded Idella of how much she had given these children by giving them her time, love, and so much nurturing. I reminded her of the impact she had on these children and that God had used her to mold, shape, and create these tiny creations that were before us. She teared up again. Idella told me of times when she held them through sickness and sadness but never tried to take the place of their mother and always reminded them that their mother and father should always come before Idella.

This very rounded, joyful, God-loving woman had the simplest of needs, pure love. I shared with her that her gift of loving children would not be wasted and that God would use her again and again and again. And that only God could point her in the direction she would go. My heart broke. I somehow knew Idella's time with these children would be coming to an end, and I could only imagine the parting scene of tears, mounting pain, and yes, the separation that only God could fill.

You see God was reaching out to Idella that very second to bring her comfort, peace and assurance that He would be her guiding force. We parted at the end of the class with only Idella looking back at me with those eyes of sadness screaming out for me to pray for her to have strength, courage, and yes, obedience. As we exchanged tearful good-byes, we were both forever changed and in awe of how powerful God really is. That burning love Idella carried so deeply in her heart for those children was uniquely orchestrated by the very hands of the Master, and only a God of love could fill her again and again and again. *I tell you the truth, Jesus replied, "no one who has left home or brothers or sisters or mother or father or children or fields for me and the gospel will fail to receive a hundred times as much in this present age and with them, and in the age to come, eternal life. Mark 10:29-30.*

As I walked to the car, my heart became so completely overjoyed with such a feeling that God had used a simple conversation to turn uncertainty in this woman's life into a complete and full reminder of how much she had given and how God was so pleased with her sacrificial service not only to those children, but to the Lord God Himself. My joy was unexplainable, and I couldn't imagine my life without having met Idella. Suddenly the choice that was made in the Spirit to go to that extra gymnastics class was no longer irrational, a time-waster, and nonsense; it was simply divine. God will never waste your time!

As we continued going to gymnastics class week after week after week, God intervened and allowed many conversations to flow in His love. Some were conversations of just pleasure and some were conversations of the divine nature. As I look back, I see that when we ask the Lord in prayer for direction, He is sure to give it, but it's up to us to follow it in faith. Those choices in life that are made in faith while holding the Father's hand produce an overwhelming joy and an abundance of goodness and a lifetime of riches. As for me, I prefer chocolate on everything including my choices! Dipped heavily!

Chapter 4

Hitchin' a Ride

W ould you be willing to give up anything the Lord asked you to give up? What if that meant giving up your car? How would you survive? Would God really ask someone to do that? I believe that in God's infinite wisdom He lovingly asks us to do things that may seem irrational, illogical, and completely without our understanding. It is up to us whether we take the risk and see what God has in store for us or spend our lives wondering what could have happened if we would had done things God's way. I'm not much of a risk-taker, but when it comes to God, there are no risks! It's always best His way no matter the circumstances.

My husband and I had been in prayer for quite some time for a couple who were having some financial struggles. We continued to pray and knew that God would help them find a way to survive. What we didn't know is that God would ask us to sell our car to help them. Our conversation with God went something like this,

Just tell us, and we'll do it.

Simple as that prayer sounds, that's all it took for God to reach out and confirm over and over again that we should sell our second car and give the proceeds to our brother in need. Selling our second car might sound like a courageous act of kindness, but it wasn't because in our hearts we just figured God would provide another car for us as that one would eventually have to be replaced anyway. Human logic doesn't exactly line up with Godly wisdom, as we soon found out.

We put the car up for sale, and within days a lady called to talk to me about the car. A very timid voice on the other end of the phone told me, "Hello." Her name was Marcella. Marcella didn't ask me to lower the price of the car; she told me that she wanted the car but needed more time to raise enough money. She asked if I would "hold" the car until the next week so she could come up with the extra money. I was shocked. I wondered why she didn't ask me to lower the price of the car but she didn't. I felt the Lord working deeply inside this conversation, so I stepped aside and allowed the Holy Spirit to work.

My heart was deeply softened by this woman who proclaimed she loved the car and confessed to not even driving it! I couldn't believe it. She went on to tell me that she had been praying that the Lord would provide her with a car so she could find a job, and when she passed by my Dad's yard and saw the car for sale, something told her to stop even though she figured the car would be too expensive for her. She said she felt my Dad's spirit telling her the truth about the car and if he said it was a good old car, then she didn't need to drive it. I was shocked at how God was working to bless us both!

I could feel the Spirit of the Lord falling on this conversation with each word spoken. At that moment if the Lord had not already designated that money to go to our brother in need, the car would have been Marcella's with only exchanging God's love. But God's plan was different. I asked Marcella how much money she had for the car and she told me how much she had saved, down to the penny. I told her we would take that exact amount for the car. Marcella proclaimed how good God was to her with each jump for joy!!! Oh no, it wasn't excitement for the price going down, it was excitement for the Lord's hand who had provided for her. God had chosen that specific moment to join the hands of those who love Him and share His riches and abundant blessings. And with that we said goodbye and waited for God to provide another car for us.

Someone should have yelled at me, "God's getting ready to

teach you something," when we became a one-car family. At first we didn't even notice we only had one car, odd as that sounds. Both my husband and I both had already quit our jobs, anticipating our move and neither one of us had to commute to work. I thought it would be a breeze. God's ever present signature was stamped on the next phase of what we call "Hitchin a' Ride".

Suddenly our schedules began to crash! I needed the car to get the children back and forth to school, preschool parties, meetings, end of the year field trips, (with the dozens of mommy miles racked up running for the kids,) not to mention trying to fit in seeing friends and family before we left. My husband's errands suddenly became emergency after emergency the closer we got to moving day, and then it erupted! A little door was opened in our relation-ship that was filled with frustration, lack of communication, anger, resentment, poor planning, and lack of consideration. Oh yes, Satan was making his presence known through the suddenly unhappy situation of having to share a car. Frequently you could hear at least one of us saying on any given day, ... "But, I've got to have the car!" or "You didn't tell me you needed the car for that day!" The conversations became more heated, and yes, we became more and more frustrated with each other and ultimately questioned God on why He had not yet provided another car.

You see, whenever we make a mess of things, God is ever present and ready to provide a way out, if we are willing to listen and obey. That's it listen and obey. So on our knees we went, our conversation with God went something like this,

Lord, we know your plan is best for us. But we can't make this work. We are failing miserably at sharing one car between both of us with two kids that have different schedules and school. The errands are coming faster than speeding bullets, and, yes, we are frustrated. We cry out to you for forgiveness. We have missed something. We have missed a blessing. What is it, Lord? What have we missed? Teach us, Lord. What are you trying to teach us?

We heard nothing from God. He chose to remain completely silent on the issue. We frequently prayed for another car, but month after month God chose not to provide it. We accepted it, and from that moment forward my husband and I both decided to do it God's way. If it's to be one car, then so be it. That was only the beginning of one of the richest stories I've ever been a part of where two people learn that doing things God's way produces things humans cannot. *The heart of the discerning acquires knowledge; the ears of the wise seek it out. Proverbs 18: 15.*

God taught us through the struggles of sharing one car to relinquish all pride. It wasn't easy to admit to the world that you have to "ask for the car" but we did just that. And we learned to ask for help when we needed it, which is also a big pride breaker. But the real lesson from God came very early one Saturday morning when my husband had to be in one place and our youngest daughter had to be somewhere else at the same time. My husband was forced to hitch-a-ride with a friend to class.

During the ride to class, God began speaking to my husband through an acquaintance named Tom. David and Tom began talking about sharing a car and how hard that was, when the Holy Spirit took over and revealed to David God's truths and God's blessings loud and clear. Tom pointed out that David and I must have great communication with each other and complete selflessness in order to share a car. Also, that our every thought each day seemed to be on the other person and his or her needs and how that must have enriched our relationship, our communication, our love for each other and, yes, the very foundation of our marriage. WOW! How could we have missed that big of a God lesson? God had blessed us more than we could imagine and we totally missed it!! Our relationship had changed right before our very eyes, and we couldn't even see it. Our conversation with God went something like this,

Lord, you always provide in abundance even when we can't see it's in abundance. We have grown in our marriage and our relationship and, yes, we talk more, we give more, we are willing to put the other person first; and, yes, we are more flexible with each other and had we not had to share this car, I don't think we would be sitting here this very second praising you for the growth our marriage has taken. WOW! Your love is so powerful. We can only see a tiny, tiny part of our lives, but you, Lord God, can see the entire picture and all, I mean all, of our needs. You have provided things we didn't even ask you for! We are so in awe of how great you are, Lord God. And if we need to keep hitchin-a-ride, then that's just fine!

Chapter 5

Bus Stop Momma

Often times things that begin very simply are things that God intends for them to stay that way. God puts certain events in our lives in a sequence that we can't make sense of nor should we. The story of Bus Stop Momma is one of those situations that don't make sense but somehow I gained a peace about it as the Lord so lovingly reached out one day and changed my name.

After many months of struggling to find my fit after leaving the business world and being thrown full-force into being a full time wife and mom, I found myself trying to be something I'm wasn't. A friend often shared her childhood experiences with me about her own mother, and it gave me such a warm, loving feeling with almost a glow.

I began thinking about what type of mom my friend Deanna had growing up, and I wanted nothing but the best for my children and wondered how I could be more like her own mom. Deanna described this place she called home as being filled with love and honesty, almost like being swallowed up in a blanket of security! She describes her mom as the "King-Dong Mom." The "King Dong Mom" got her name from that precious moment the little girl came home from school, and there waiting for her was not only mom's arms but the King-Dong perfectly placed upon the napkin. This house wasn't filled only with loving parents but with an ever-steady force of servantship to the Lord and dedication to giving this child all of her needs spiritually and emotionally and physically. Her Christ-centered, nurturing environment enveloped her in this nest of comfort, security, and happiness. That nurturing, done in such a Christ-driven, methodical order, had brought forth a child into adulthood who was self-assured, positive, funny, caring, enthusiastic, motivated, joyful, fun loving, God fearing, and full of Jesus.

My thoughts were, hey, I need to be a "King Dong Mom". So off I went trying to be a King Dong Mom! It didn't work! Oh, I could easily have had the King Dong's waiting when the kids got home, but somehow I knew I was trying to become this "model", "specimen", "person" that I clearly was not. My conversation with God went something like this,

Lord, my plan is not working. I need direction. I feel such pressure to be perfect all of the time. I feel such need to do better than any other mom has ever done. Please give me guidance.

And in the very quietness of my heart, I heard the Lord speak to me and His conversation with me went something like this,

My child, it is well. It is truly well. You must release the past and forgive where forgiveness is needed. You will develop your role as a stay-at-home mom with these things- consistent love, dedication to a self-less life, following my every command, and a consistent prayer life for you and your husband and your children.

The Lord promptly put Proverbs 31 in front of me. I took the time to read it slowly, carefully and with my pen firmly in hand. *She sets about her work vigorously; her arms are strong for her tasks. Proverbs 31:17. She is clothed with strength and dignity; she can laugh at the days to come. She speaks with wisdom, and faithful instruction is on her tongue. She watches over the affairs of her household and does not eat the bread of idleness. Her children arise and call her blessed; her husband also, and he praises her. Proverbs 31: 25-28.* After allowing Proverbs 31 to sink deep into my mind, I knew I needed more so I got down on my knees and pleaded for answers.

The Lord began lifting my burden and gave me strength, resilience, power, determination, will, and a plan that was uniquely right for me, to nurture my own family. My plan may not be right for you; only God the Father knows His unique plan for you. Trying to make someone else's plan fit into your life simply won't work. We are far too different and far too valuable for that! God loves us so much that He alone has our plan and He alone can work masterful change and give us wisps of vision until the entire picture is evident to us.

God reached out that day and gave me a plan to be an ever-present strength for my children, their greatest prayer warrior, and, yes, be present at the bus stop morning and afternoon regardless of the busyness of the day. So with that, I left my prayer closet knowing that I wasn't going to be the "King Dong Mom" because God's plan for me was a bit different.

The next day started off very early, and as I was struggling to get going, I felt these quiet words penetrate my heart that went something like this....come on Bus Stop Momma, it's time to go. And with that, I was commissioned "Bus Stop Momma", a title I proudly wear and cherish as I wait for the bus to meander up and down the streets.

I believe one of the most loving lessons the Lord has taught me was to stop trying to be someone else's mom and just be myself regardless if I am a stay-at-home mom or a mom that works outside of the home. Have faith to know that the Lord can guide you to be the mom He wants you to be no matter the difficulty, trial, and circumstance or even the past you may have had. It is Jesus alone who can change your innermost thoughts to be Christ-centered, even when the kids look like they've never had a bit of discipline in their lives! It is Jesus who can take a strained or even broken relationship with a child and rebuild it, strengthen it, and make it more solid and rooted than ever before. It is Jesus alone who can remove the hurt and the pain and bring forth a brand new creation in Christ who returns the love you give out. And it is Jesus alone who can make you the mom that is uniquely pleasing to God. And the blessings of complete obedience as a parent will multiply and grow and provide much more of a foundation for our children than we could ever do on our own.

Every time I see those big doors of that yellow school bus open, I thank God that I have been given the opportunity to be waiting at the curve and how pleased I am to be "Bus Stop Momma". It's simply the best title I've ever had!!

Chapter 6

Hazel

Would the Lord ever call us to just sit back and relax when our circumstances are in chaos? Can we exercise the amount of patience the Lord desires us to exercise when He so lovingly reaches out to teach us in His love and mercy? How can we, as children of God, take the true measure of patience He desires us to have and be still, quiet, and comfortable? *That fading flower, his glorious beauty, set on the head of a fertile valley, will be like a fig ripe before harvest-as soon as someone sees it and takes it in his hand, he swallows it. Isaiah 28:4.*

Waiting for the harvest can be one of the most challenging things God calls us to do for Him. Those periods of waiting, whether it's waiting on a job or waiting on a business opportunity or just waiting for God to provide resources can produce restlessness, feelings of abandonment, numerous bouts with doubt and shame, and most all a separation from God. But God in His infinite love and arms of tender compassion stretches our circumstances out for our good and allows us to wait to draw nearer to Him.

Drawing nearer to God was exactly what my husband did as he opened his business and began preparing to do the Lord's work in that business. David spent long hours and many nights, month after month, trying to get the business off the ground with no success. My husband turned to the Lord to find out why the business was not coming to fruition. *But seek first his kingdom and his righteousness and all these things will be given to you as well. Matthew 6:33.* As familiar as that verse was, it was a critical turning point for us as we continued to seek God's will for David's business. We enlisted prayer from one of our most trusted prayer partners, John David Stewart.

Both my husband and I had talked to John David on several occasions during this period in which the business clearly wasn't getting off the ground and his advice was solid, grounded in God's word, and clear as a bell until he said one thing- *Hazel.* John David used a very old television show called *Hazel* to make a vivid point of how God works patience and perseverance in the lives of His servants.

We were deeply distraught that God wasn't allowing David's business to fully operate. The resources were not being provided and many other things that he needed to operate were not yet available. John David told us that David was trying to run the business from his own power and make things happen in David's time and not God's time. He went on to share with us that not letting God be in control of that business had choked off the flow of blessings. Then he shocked us when he told us to lock the doors of the business, shut them down tight, turn off the lights, and tell God that whenever He was ready for this business to open, it would be fine with us. He went on to tell us to cry out to God that we would be faithful to wait it out no matter how long it might take. Patience with a big P!

At that point, it sounded like an absurd idea to lock down the business that God led my husband to open and walk away from it. Let the phone ring, let the faxes come in, and leave everything alone. But somehow my husband and I both felt that God was speaking to us loudly and clearly and trying to teach us a lesson of patience and trust for our sole provisions. We allowed God's truth to ring in our ears. After we survived the initial shock of shutting down the business, John David then told us jokingly to sit back, relax, and watch a little bit of Hazel. We all laughed out loud! We pondered the concept of "Hazel" – it was not appealing! So we went to the Lord in prayer and our conversation with the Lord went something like this,

Lord, give us guidance and melt our hearts to your will.

I walked out of that prayer time knowing God's will was about to appear right before my eyes. David knew too without a shadow of a doubt that *Hazel* was becoming a reality. We spent some time on our knees asking God to confirm what we both really knew to be true, and He did loudly and clearly. At first, our hearts both saddened. But we knew that it wasn't going to work unless God had full control, we were ready to make that leap. David picked up his large frame, bent over in sorrow, and made that walk to his office. He turned the door handle slowly and peeped in. He methodically turned his computer off and didn't bother to go through the mountain of paperwork on his desk screaming for attention. With that he flipped the light off and very solemnly shut the door. The sound of the door shutting was prominent, satisfying, and saddening all at the same time. There was an eerie silence in the room. I watched as my love, my best friend, my mate displaced himself out of his own business while I stood there helplessly wondering how I could soften the blow. I didn't know whether to talk or be silent. We sat outside his office and just looked at the double doors that pressed the business closed. I wanted to put a sign out that said, "Closed, by order of my Lord and Savior- will reopen when God sees fit." But nothing remained on the door except our feelings of helplessness, restlessness, and despair. We walked away, neither one of us speaking. Words could not begin to describe how hollow our hearts felt as we walked away from a business that we felt was commissioned by the Lord. The business was not important at that point and neither was any thought of our finances. It was God who was on our minds. How we must have disappointed Him so when we tried to make it happen in our time. Our conversation with God went something like this:

Oh Lord, we need you. We need to feel your very breath of life in our weakened bodies. We give this business to you completely for you to either open it or never open it again. It's in your care; not ours. We submit to you, Lord God, and you are our one and only Master. You are our Savior, our Redeemer and our Comforter. Bring us comfort in this decision. Bring us peace in walking away. Bring us joy from serving you in this manner. Let no division come between us in this decision. Bind up the enemy from attacking our thoughts and telling us to get in there and work before it is truly your time. It feels unnatural, God. Help it to feel natural because it is part of your plan for our lives at this very second. We don't know if you'll ever open this business again, but it is well either way. We just want to love you and adore you. You are the only thing that matters to us, Lord God, and only you can establish the work of our hands. You do that in your own time and it will be fine. Forgive us for attacking your business with every ounce of strength we've had. It was not your plan. Our attacking this business day and night has proven to be nothing good or useful. So we give it to you this very day and say thank you, Lord, for the forgiveness, mercy, and love you so awesomely show us. And Lord, I think we'll go watch a little "Hazel" until we hear from you.

Well for you *Hazel fans*, you'll be saddened to find out that after only two days, the Lord saw fit to open up David's business fully. Just two days, and the business opened up! Imagine that; David had tried for months and months to make things happen and in just two days of submitting to God's will, bam, the business up and running, but this time on God's power. Opposition that David faced was suddenly broken down, lack of resources melted away, David began to see future business opportunities and ultimately he was provided more than he ever expected. *So I saw that there is nothing better for a man than to enjoy his work, because that is his lot.* Ecclesiastes 3:22a. David simply had nothing more on his mind than just jumping in there and enjoying the work that God had given him.

Shutting down the business and giving God full control was only one component because you might think that at that specific point in time, the business began to prosper and David began a season of reaping. That truly was not the case. God was calling David into another period of patience and perseverance in which he worked diligently with the resources that God had provided. But the fruit of his effort would not be seen until over a year later. How would you like to get up each day and go into a job and work diligently and prayerfully, seek God's wisdom each day and not get paid for over a year? Would that produce a measure of patience in you that you might not have had before? God's wisdom cannot be understood by human wisdom. *But God has revealed to us in his Spirit. The Spirit teaches all things, even the deep things of God. For who among men knows the thoughts of man except the man's spirit within him? In the same way no one knows the thoughts of God except the Spirit of God. We have not received the spirit of the world but the Spirit who is from God that we may understand what God has freely given us. That is what we speak, not in words taught us by human wisdom but in words taught by the Spirit, expressing spiritual truths in spiritual words. I Corinthians 2:10-13*

In our human wisdom we could not understand the purpose of that season of waiting for the business to take off, but we developed patience with God and began to relax. We were secure that every good and perfect thing from the Father takes a measure of trust that only the Holy Spirit can provide. As the Holy Spirit provided trust, anxiety fell away, tension disappeared, and turmoil ceased. Sweet!

Do not mistake this example of God working in our lives for advice to shut your business down or quit your job or make a serious life change without specifically being directed by the Holy Spirit to do so. For us, the Lord gave us great assurance that we were acting in his Spirit, and we fell flat into the arms of a loving God!

Our Conversations with God

On Trust

Chapter 7

A Very Different Christmas

The holidays bring such a variety of things to do that it has become a challenge to even fit in the basics reason for this celebration of life- it is Christ. There are cookies to bake, presents to buy, school plays, musicals and festivities to attend, in addition to the enormous need of spending time with our families and friends, near and far. There are trips to plan, people to see, and just when you think you've gotten all of the gifts under the tree, you find yourself back in the store for just one more. Christmas and all that it brings has made us so busy that it's very easy to take the Christ out of Christmas without even knowing it. *For to us a child is born, to us a son is given, and the government shall be on his shoulders. And he will be called Wonderful Counselor, Mighty God, Everlasting Father, Prince of Peace. Isaiah 9:6.* I'm convinced that God the Father rejoices in our celebration of His Son's birth. Wouldn't it be glorious if we could look to our heavenly Father during a holiday season and hear Him say to us, "Well done thy good and faithful servant!"

One particular year, the Lord looked down on our family and chose something very different for our Christmas celebration. It was a year that we have never forgotten and a year that brought the depth of the season bursting in our hands as our hearts were warmed to celebrating the birth of Christ through the eyes of the

Father. This very different Christmas began with our resources being depleted in the month of December. We simply could not buy gifts for our family or friends, and the most grieving part was that we could not buy for our children as we desired. Our conversation with God went something like this,

Lord, Lord you know that we have sacrificed for you. But our children won't even have a Christmas this year. We can't buy for them. Our hearts are so sad. Lord, reach out your hand and bless our children this Christmas. We can't buy for them and they are so little. We simply cannot bear the pain of not giving to our children. Help us to see this through your eyes, Lord!

In that very moment we felt the Lord speaking and His conversation with us went something like this,

Your children will have the richest Christmas season they have ever known. Trust me, and I shall provide for all of your needs this season.

As the days were marked off on the calendar, Christmas was approaching, and we couldn't see anything materially that was going to be provided for our children for Christmas. So we decided to just dig in and trust God that He knew what was best for our children. On this very different Christmas there was no tree in the house to decorate. That was odd. There were no lights to string. That was unusual. There were no cookies to bake. That felt unnatural. There were very few presents to wrap. That seemed impossible. There were simply no tasks demanding our attention except for attending a few school plays and our Christmas music at church. It was the simplest of Christmases that I've ever seen. We didn't fight traffic or fight the crowds at the malls for shopping, and we found ourselves gathered together as a family loving each other and spending so much time getting to know the heart of the Lord. We huddled around the fire, and even though there was the absence of the prominent Christmas tree in the room, we focused on what we did have. We looked around and saw no chaos, only peace and love.

We used this time to fall deep into prayer with the Lord as our children asked for nothing. We were free to relax and enjoy the season for the very first time.

As we drew closer to Christmas, the Lord was so kind to allow our children to receive a few gifts from very unexpected sources. Suddenly our girls were blessed with little, unexpected Christmas gifts. People that we barely knew gave to our children. Mere acquaintances handed gifts to our girls as we watched in awe of what God does when we allow Him to fully control of our lives. But the most lavish, the most exquisite and the most cherished present of all was yet to come.

I went to the Lord in prayer thanking the Father for giving us so much this Christmas season, and God allowed me to see through His eyes and His heart for just a brief and fleeting moment. I envisioned the heavenly Father placing into both of my hands a finely crafted wooden box with a lid fitting on top of the box. I didn't open the box but somehow I knew it was our Christmas gift from the Lord lying in that box. I still did not open the box; I held it tightly in my hands. The box was heavy and appeared to be very full. I was curious but remained still. I pictured God coming down from His throne and removing the lid off the box very slowly and carefully, reaching in and pulling out what appeared to be a very large gemstone that was sparkling with brilliance and appeared to be almost blue in color. He told me to take the gemstone in my hand. I couldn't hold it with one hand - it took both hands and then I looked deep inside the gemstone and found the gift. Inside this particular gemstone was the gift of satisfied children. As the Lord took another gemstone out and had me look into it, it was the gift of a loving mate. Tears streamed down my face as I looked to the Father in awe of how much he had given me this Christmas season. As I looked to Him, I could not speak. His question to me was, "How much do you think the gift of satisfied children is worth?" I could not answer. I envisioned God on His heavenly throne replying, "It is priceless, no amount of money can buy that. It is simply priceless." Then another question He posed to me, "What would the richest man in the world pay for a loving mate?" Again I could not speak. He replied, "There aren't enough coins in the world for that, it's simply priceless." I stood there in the Lord's loving splendor and couldn't imagine how valuable the box I was holding was. And somehow I knew that for each Christmas to come, our family would be blessed by the fountain of love flowing out of the heart of the Lord as I held these gemstones of God delicately in my mind. It was simply our gift for keeping Christ in Christmas.

Christmas, Christmas, Christmas

The season is here and all that we hold dear
is your love Lord God, your presence and
yes your Son that guides this day to cheer.

You alone are Christmas and you alone are near.
Even when the world says no, you Lord God have
the mightiest hand in all of the land.

As others seek to take the Christ out of Christmas,
my heart knows the truth and my prayers turn to you
for them to see you, love you and long for the Christ in Christmas.

The season is filled with such color and adornment.
The trees of spruce stamp you are God.
The trees of fir confirm you are Lord.
The trees of pine let us know we were firmly on your mind.

As the trees are adorned with lights and color of the season
they cannot shine without you Lord God behind each one
of bright bringing them into your Son's light.

You alone are Christmas.
You alone are Christ.
It is after all the Christ in Christmas that delivers the day,
brings life to the world and breath to this nation.

That is the only reason we can say it is truly Christmas Day
is to keep you at the front of Christmas and have your Son as Christ.

All others who seek to make you second or take you out crucify
again without even a shout.

It is Christmas and you Lord God ring the bell with fullness
and joy as we stand firm that Christ is Christmas in the Father,
the Son and the Holy Ghost.
The three that set this time apart will be for the whole nation
to see that Christmas, Christmas, Christmas is truly the God given
Trinity!!!!!

God, the Father, has such magnificent plans for our lives if we
allow Him to reign and rule over every day of our lives, including
the holidays. Our children learned to breathe Christ into the season.
David and I cherished the fact that we deeply, deeply loved each
other more than we ever realized and that Christ alone is the celebration. It took the hand of the Lord allowing our resources to be
depleted for us to receive one of the biggest blessings in life.

Our very different Christmas shines so bright as we look back in
time and I can't imagine what we would have missed out on if we
had not sought the Lord in prayer that night. Tiny prayers of simple
thanks to a loving Father produced a wealth of love, contentment,
rejoicing, peace and basking in His greatness. That is prayer at its
finest. *I will be glad and rejoice I you; I will sing praise to your
name, O Most High. Psalm 9:2.*

That very different Christmas sprinkled with a measure of trust,
a gallon of contentment, and an infinite supply of love for a truly
Christ centered Christmas cannot be obtained anywhere but at the
throne of Jesus! That was the very merriest of times!!

Chapter 8

The Road up the Mountain

Twisting and turning and trusting God every step of the way was far, far from our minds one very innocent Friday evening. The Lord used the elements of nature, His lesson of love, and, yes, the road up the mountain to show us about trust and His unfailing love.

Strange as it may seem the Lord had given me the gift of being comfortable driving in the mountains. The Lord removed the fear that I had initially about moving to a mountain by giving me a peace about the place where He has called us to live. That can only be from the hand of a loving, giving God who gives a believer something he doesn't even know he needs. It was totally out of character for me to be so calm, relaxed, and, yes, confident about the mountain after living in the same place all of my life, especially since it is anything but mountainous in the state of Louisiana!

The mountain itself is so beautiful beyond belief. When we look around, we see how God's hand has painted the nighttime sky that begins to turn pale blue before sunset. We see streams that flow between the mountains that have the most sparkling, crystal white water we've ever seen. The forest is deeply rich in greens, and the hills flow upward and downward, winding around valleys and turning inward and outward offering breath-taking views from mountaintop to mountaintop. We see a massive river of power and force flowing in tune to God's command, and yet the setting is so peaceful, so serene, so full of God's hand. What a magnificent city for God's people to soak up, bask in, and see His majestic landscape stretching over the land.

The mountain view simply cannot be copied, reproduced, multiplied, removed, or seen from any place other than the mountain itself. Living in a setting which feels like God's love being poured out all over us each day makes it hard to imagine that the road we took one innocent Friday evening turned into a pathway of sheer panic, terror, horror, disbelief, trembling, doubt, and massive amounts of fear combined into one feeling all at the same time.

The wind blew softly that evening as my husband and daughters took to the open road. We had just finished a dinner and decided we needed to run some errands off the mountain. So we took off without a thought. We generally plan our schedules, errands, and trips off the mountain very carefully; this time we did not. We went shopping and ran our errands and noticed that is was beginning to rain. This was a welcome sight since we had been in nearly drought conditions for most of the summer. Innocently my husband got behind the wheel, the baby buckled securely in her car seat, and our other daughter and I strapped in and ready to go. Off we went. As we traveled further down the highway, it began to rain harder and harder. My husband slowed down considerably and began trying to wipe his glasses to see. My daughter began to fidget in the back seat and then said, "Dad, can you see?" He slowed the car even more with the glare on his glasses giving him fits; he admitted he could not see well. He went a bit farther and then pulled over and said, "Susan, you need to drive." I knew it was serious for him to ask for help. I hesitated but then jumped over into the driver's seat and took off very slowly.

The wind and the rain still pelted the car, but we pressed forward. I was just thankful that there was a car ahead of me to help me see the road, as it was pretty dark and there were no reflectors in sight. We continued on very slowly and carefully as the baby was chattering in the background about the bolts of lightening that were illuminating the nighttime sky. Then the time came. We started up the mountain road.

I was still feeling very confident. We proceeded up the mountain, and I began to slow down. The rain was fierce. The winds were howling. My windshield wipers were going at full force, my vision was somewhat impaired but I still had a good idea of where the turns were. There were no cars in front of me this time to help guide me up the mountain. I was on my own or so I thought. There was a string of cars behind me. I tried to ignore them. I slowed the car again as the rain worsened. There were no pull offs and no way off the road. I thought to myself that I just had to keep moving and make it up the mountain. I made a turn around a very long curve about halfway up the mountain and then it hit; the clouds were hovering heavily on the mountain. The clouds frequently hovered over the mountain when it rained, but this time it was different. These were massive clouds that left visibility slim to none. I could not see at all. I slowed the car to nearly stopping. I sat upright and my husband told me I was getting close to the edge. My daughter was praying in the backseat. There was tension in the air. The rain was pounding; my heart was racing. I had no vision at all! It was equivalent to closing my eyes and just guessing where the turns were. For the moment I was blinded! I knew there was a turn coming up, but I couldn't see it. I cried out to the Lord, "Help me! I can't see! I can't stop. I can't go. I can't see. Help me!" In my vision was total darkness, and then a bolt of lightening illuminated my way to show me the curve ahead. I made it through the curve. My fingers clutched the steering wheel, with my eyes opened as wide as they could get; still I couldn't see. Another bolt of lightening lit my way. "Thank you, Lord." I knew there were three more major passes I had to get through to make it to the top. Fear was racing through my body. One wrong move, and it wouldn't be good. I couldn't make a mistake. I couldn't feel my heart anymore. Terror overwhelmed me. I prayed, "Please, Lord, give me another bolt of lightening. I can't make it through these passes without vision." We made pass number one and climbed higher. We began pass number two, and I nearly stopped; I couldn't see! God once again lit the sky for me. We made it through pass number two. We neared the top and made it through pass number three, and though we approached the edge of the mountain so closely, God's hand was still upon us. We crept upward, and then we pulled to the top! All in the car cheered with joy! My daughter screamed with excitement, "Mom, you did it!" I caught my breath. My heart was still pounding. We arrived home after many other twists and turns and hills, and then I stopped the car. I couldn't move. My hands were concreted to the steering wheel. My feet were made of lead. Fear had paralyzed me. I sat there and then asked God what had just happened and why He let us go through that horror. Feeling His infinite kindness and merciful love, I recalled a soft delicate scripture- *Never will I leave you; never will I forsake you. Hebrews 13:5b.*

I was still puzzled and in a slight daze, and my conversation with God went something like this,

What lesson were we to learn Father? What lesson?

As I continued over and over to seek God to find out what we were to learn from that road up the mountain, I knew that God certainly knew of the conditions, and yet He allowed us to go through them. They could have shaken our faith, lessened our confidence, and sent us tumbling downward in a spiral of fear and doubt about living on the mountain. They did none of those. God chooses to allow us to go through things that will awaken our faith, lead us out of times of trouble, and teaches us that when there is no way, He will make a way.

On that treacherous trip up the mountain, it taught me that God is the ruler of every detail of our lives. Had we consulted him on our plans for the evening, I'm not sure if they would have been any different or not. I cannot question that. I do know this- even though the situation was terrifying, I still clung to the bolts of lightening that illuminated the darkened sky to make our way. Had there been no bolts of lightening, God would have made some other way for us to see. God doesn't intend for his children to be lost and wandering around in the darkness. Even if we know Him, we can still be blind to His love, His power, His mercy, and, yes, His very own provisions. Quite often God provides but we live in darkness because He has not provided the way we think He should have provided. The enemy is the one who is blinding us to that. Satan wants you and me to believe that God has forsaken us and that He has not provided at all. That is a lie! *The works of his hands are faithful and just and his precepts are trustworthy, they are steadfast forever and ever, done in faithfulness and uprightness. Psalm 111:7-8.* The key is trust. It is one simple word that requires us to put our total faith in God. We should not question the circumstances we are in but trust that God will provide for *all* of our needs regardless of the road we are on.

If we had had our way on that fearful night, the rains would have cleared on the road up the mountain, our trip would have been meaningless, and we would have remained in total control. But that simply wasn't God's way. While our plans went awry, God's plans were certain, sure, and definite. We learned that even in the midst of the fiercest storm, God's still required us to trust Him even with our very own lives- and to know that He loves us. He knew how our road up the mountain would end even before it began. He provided everything we needed, in those terrifying moments, and as we left the car we knew in the midst of darkness, there will always, always be one guiding force of light on or off that ole' mountain road!

Chapter 9

Dollars and No Sense

God's provisions can often shock us and bless us and even startle us at times. Looking back on our past provisions is easy. It may have been a new job, healthcare, or even a home that we could point a finger at and say beyond a shadow of a doubt that God provided those things in our lives. But would God give us provisions that are shocking, startling or even devastating? What happens when we can't see God's provisions for the future? God loves us so much that He desires our total dependence on Him for *all* of our provisions. God took our needs for our family and listened to our prayers and wove them together with His hands of infinite love and came up with a financial plan for our lives that was shocking, intriguing, and so humbling.

As my husband and I sat silently one evening knowing that our financial future was about to be changed and put totally and completely into the Lord's hands, we became very still before the Lord. We were scared. We were unsure. We needed to hear how we would survive. The Holy Spirit was so specific when he called my husband and me to quit our jobs. But what we didn't hear or see or feel was how we would survive financially. Our family was being swept up into a whirlwind, moved into a land we had not seen, and yes, told to open a business that neither of us could fully comprehend in God's plan.

Question after question came to our minds about our financial future. In our minds our savings would only last so long. We could see our resources being used to move and open the business; we couldn't see any financial future at all. Were we still in God's love and God's care? Did God show us how to survive without jobs or income? Would God be there to help us survive following His good and perfect will? How could we survive this type of total financial dependence on God? Time and time again my husband and I pondered those nagging questions and how it just didn't make any sense at all, for a married couple to leave perfectly good jobs. It just didn't make sense at all but God had such a massive plan for our future including our finances that He wanted our attention. He got it! *He has showed you, O man what is good. And what does the Lord require of you? To act justly and to love mercy and to walk humbly with your God. Micah 6:8* Our conversation with God went something like this,

Lord, we just can't see what's ahead, but we know that you will always guard us and love us and never harm us. Take our finances, our savings, and whatever other resources you have for us in the future and guide us. Let us make not one purchase without your stamp of approval from a simple carton of milk up to the place we are to live. You make the decision and give us wisdom to follow your guidance. Remove the enemy's presence from our thought, and our minds, and replace the fear and doubt with trust for your perfect plan. Help our children to understand that our money is no longer ours but truly yours. Help us to learn the lessons you want us to learn from this time in our lives when we feel we truly need dollars and it make no sense. For you are good and merciful and perfect in every way and will never make a mistake. Guide us. Protect us and lead us into our financial future whatever that may be.

And it was with that prayer that the Lord began providing a peace about not having jobs, opening a business with no visible source of income to live on. Our job was to simply be patient and wait on the Lord to guide us and provide for us. *Be patient, then brothers, until the Lord's coming. See how the farmer waits for the land to yield the valuable crop and how patient he is for the autumn and spring rains. You too, be patient and stand firm, because the Lord's coming is near. James 5:7-8.*

We began our season of waiting and rested comfortably in God's arms. But patience, especially financial patience is terribly difficult. It can produce times of anger, bitterness, envy, jealousy and hatred. The enemy was ever present each time the checkbook was balanced and we saw nothing but money going out and nothing coming in and no sign of anything coming in for the future either! Our joy was robbed, our happiness sheared off, and our dependence on God shaken. Our checkbook balance dwindled down to what we thought was critically low, and we were afraid. Should we look for jobs? Our questioning God's plan for our financial future did nothing less than slap God in the face and tell Him we were jumping ship because this thing was going down! Oh how merciful God was to us! Oh how His hand of love reached out to rescue us each time we feared that we would not make it. Oh how soft and gentle His touch of love was whenever He comforted us. And yes, oh how God's provisions surprised us again and again. God's provisions were wound so tightly in His love that when we trusted God for our livelihood and our very existence, He blessed us beyond comprehension. But getting there was an upward climb, and climb we did!

We continued to see no visible source of income in our future. We continued to spend money on food, clothing, shelter, and the basic necessities of life. My husband was strictly in charge of spending the money God had entrusted him with and I can honestly say that every dime spent was carefully done so in prayer and supplication to God.

My oldest daughter commented one day about something she wanted to buy for school, and without evening knowing it, she had changed her whole thinking on money and spending. Her usual comment would have been something like, "Mom, I need this for school. Give me a check." But now her tone, her words, and her asking were quite different. "Mom, could you ask Dad to pray about this and tell me if I can get this for school?" WOW! What a miracle, God! I had seen how the Lord was teaching this young girl about submission, responsibility and yes, even dependence on God for everything! I could have spent my whole life talking to her about those things, but in one sweep the Lord sent a clear message to her that our money was not our own and that He is the sole source of all things in our lives. What a tiny, little lesson from a very powerful God that impacts the lives of our children to give them the very foundation of His love.

As the hand of God continued to surprise us month after month after month we knew the time was coming. God had been preparing our hearts for a bigger test of faith than our last one, and we knew this one was serious. My husband and I both felt in our hearts that all of our savings, and all sources of any income that were left would be soon used up completely with no sight of financial relief anywhere to be found. It was coming. My conversation with a close friend confirmed it, and his advice to us was simple. "The storm is coming, get ready, stand firm in your faith, and do not be shaken. Know that God will take care of you and don't start packing up and whatever you do, don't jump ship! God will take care of you." His advice was pure, his heart was so full of truth, and his words proved ever so true!

David and I drew closer to God during this time, and as we did, we also drew closer to each other, a natural fallout and a blessing we didn't expect. My husband and I spent some time in prayer early one morning, and as we did, I envisioned us taking every single coin we had including our checkbook and giving it to the Lord. As I emptied out even the change in my purse and handed it to a merciful God, I envisioned the Lord receiving it and our checkbook with hands of care and placing it in His pocket. It was His. I spotted a single dime on the floor in our bedroom closet and as I reached down to pick it up, I also handed that dime over to the Lord. He received it and placed it in another pocket. For the very first time I truly knew the meaning of giving every last coin we had left to the Lord. Everything, everything was His. We had prayed that many times but until that very moment, I had not wholeheartedly done that. What a sweet place to be! How humbling and how very satisfying!

The Lord was preparing us for His devastating provision while giving us powerful tools in our testimony for God's love on our lives. As startling as it was, we began to see how our savings were running out, and the business was not even close to providing for our family. I prayed for my husband during that time as if he were going to war. I saturated my prayers for my husband with God's love and asked God to comfort him during this time; after all David was charged with being the provider of the family and making sure that we ate, had a place to live, and we had clothes on our backs. What an awesome responsibility, he had to be able to look into the face of God and say, "Help me!" And look into the face of God is exactly what he did day and night.

Slowly but surely the day was approaching. Fall gave away to winter and the coldest of times approached. The temperatures on the mountain were breaking records and the need for heat in the house was ever present. God continued to reassure us in gentle ways that He had His loving hands all over our circumstances.

I told my husband about a dream I had had months before the day arrived and it proved true in every way. The dream began with me flying so peacefully in the air at a certain height. Then I began to drop. I dropped some more. Then I dropped some more. Fear gripped my whole body; I feared for my life. I dropped some more. I cried out to the Lord for His hand to keep me from falling, and I dropped some more. I saw below a very soft, fluffy covering beneath me which appeared to be a cloud and the very bottom of the fall. I knew the inevitable was coming. I could see I was falling to the very bottom. I fell. But when I landed, I was cushioned by such softness and comfort that as I looked back up in to the sky, my question to God was, "How much?" I knew the bottom was using up the very last coin we had. I sighed but felt no fear and absolute peace. The Lord lifted me back up into the sky higher and higher and higher and higher until I reached the point at which I had started. Then He lifted me even higher than where I started! What an awesome way for a very loving God to graciously give me a sign in the clouds of His care for my family and me. That sign then setting us even higher than before were blessings that could only come from the hand of God.

My dream proved true as the day approached. That day I remember as being very cold outside as sleet began to fall into the nighttime hours. As my husband and I reached out to love and console each other, we grabbed our hands together and went to the Lord in prayer. Our conversation with God went something like this,

Lord, you knew this day was coming. That's it. We are completely out of money. Everything has been used up. We have no way to pay for rent, food, or anything. We look to you as being our only source of provision, and we know you have not forgotten us. So just take us and provide whenever you see fit. But, um, God, HURRY!!!!!!!!!!!!!!

We knew God was not a God of order-taking but in our flesh we felt a real urgency. We continued to pray and ask the Lord for guidance for the most basic of needs. Suddenly a $12 haircut was out of reach. It felt as odd as trying to write with my left hand, unnatural.

Within a matter of days, the Lord provided again and in the oddest of ways. Persons that were least likely (in our minds) to help us survive this trial filled our coin purse until it became full and overflowing. A struggling seminary student gave to us, a dear sweet widow gave in abundance, and a wonderful woman of faith reached out to us in a time of uncertainty of her own and gave to us! When God provides, He does it in ways unknown to man but very clearly stamps His signature over each provision, just to let us know He loves us, cares for us, and will never forsake us.

Trusting God in times of financial uncertainty brought us into a royal treasury of sorts. It allowed us a deeper access to the Father and a level of trust we never dreamed possible and prepared our hearts to do whatever the Lord called us to do financially. God is always right. His plans can be shocking, even startling sometimes but He can never make a bad decision when it comes to our finances!

And as for our dollars, they still belong to God. As for it making sense, most of the time it doesn't. That's the great part! It's when it doesn't make sense at all that God does some of his biggest miracles. We survived that trial and grew closer to God in the process. We knew that a loving and merciful God had been at close watch over our finances the entire time. What better hands to be in than the hands of the Almighty God!

Our Conversations
with God

On Loving His Way

Chapter 10

Hotcakes and Jesus

Awkward as it sounds, the title "Hotcakes and Jesus" has been deeply embedded into my soul, and it has touched the lives of so many involved directly and indirectly into a ministry of simply loving God's people. God works to bless us each and every day we wake to serve Him. That's exactly what happened one morning when I awoke and pleaded for the Lord to use me and to put someone in front of me who needed His love that day.

Simple as it sounds Gods wants to hear from us - His believers, His people- for the simplest of needs. My needs were very simple that day; I needed to be used for the Lord's glory. Not only were my needs met but many ripples of blessings were carried forth, blessings that only the hand of a loving God could manifest. *Hear, O LORD , and answer me, for I am poor and needy. Guard my life, for I am devoted to you. You are my God; save your servant who trusts in you. Have mercy on me, O Lord, for I call to you all day long. Bring joy to your servant, for to you, O Lord, I lift up my soul. Psalm 86: 1-4.*

Joy comes in so many different forms that quite often we rob ourselves of our joy when we take our focus off of Jesus and God's purpose for us each day. Joy was the last thing on my mind as I pulled up in the drive-thru line at McDonald's early one morning. What a whirlwind of a day already! God still had full control even though the chaos of the day was ever present on my mind. The busyness of getting kids off to school and getting to a doctor's appointment was wearing me down, and it was only 7:30am!

As I approached the drive-thru line, the only thing I could think of was getting a quick drink and dashing off. Breakfast was not on my mind. God had different plans. As I inched up in line I had a thought that maybe I should order some hotcakes, but then I decided that I really wasn't in the mood for hotcakes, so I dismissed the thought. As I approached the speaker to order, I felt the need again to order hotcakes, but once again said to myself, "No, I'm certainly not going to order something I'm not going to eat." Well, the Holy Spirit had different plans.

I pulled up to the speaker to order, and without hesitating I instantly ordered a medium drink and an order of hotcakes. I stopped and wondered if I had I lost my mind. Why did I say that? I'm not even in the mood for hotcakes. Oh well, I thought, maybe after I got them, they would look good, and I would be hungry for them. So I proceeded on and even went as far as taking the lid off the hotcakes to get a whiff to see if that would entice me into eating them, but it didn't work. I couldn't understand it. I bought the hotcakes and I hadn't eaten breakfast and still for some unknown reason to me I just didn't want them. In fact, I immediately placed the lid back on the hotcakes and just set them aside, not knowing what I would do with them.

I drove to work hurriedly, of course, as my day was starting off about two hours behind already and then rushed to park. If you know anything at all about downtown Baton Rouge, you know that a parking space is like gold, and the company that I was working for at the time had parking spaces but it was about 3/4 of a mile from the parking lot to the office. Well, the Lord uses even the most trying of circumstances to bless us if we allow Him. On many hot summer days in downtown Baton Rouge it was miserable to even think of walking several blocks in the heat of morning or even after-noon, but I just did it and was thankful I had a job. Our parking lot was adjacent to the parking for the courthouse and on that day parents with their children going to juvenile court were hurrying along the same path that I was taking to get to work. But on that particular walk to work, Jesus came along to answer my prayer.

I generally walked at a very fast pace to get to work and this day was no exception. I buzzed on by this tall, lanky boy about 12 years old wearing a very long pair of blue shorts that obviously were his favorite. Ahead of him walked his mom, almost pulling his slender frame to make him inch closer and closer to their destination of the day – juvenile court. As I flew by them in almost a jog with my purse flying backwards on my arm followed by a bag and of course, the bag that contained the hotcakes that were still somewhat warm, the boy resounded to his mother "...Man, mom, McDonalds, we should have gone to McDonalds for breakfast...hmmmm, man, mom." His mom, obviously aggravated with his lack of concern about getting to court on time, turned around abruptly and put her hand on her hip and told the boy that they weren't made of money and besides it was late anyway. Well, that was it for me. My race to get to work quickly ended. Jesus took over and just began speaking through me. I was just along for the ride at that point.

I dropped back and let the boy catch up with me while his mother was still a few feet ahead moving at the pace at which a mother moves when it's time to be somewhere important. I looked over at the sweet-faced boy and asked him if he liked McDonalds. He replied in a soft, gentle tone, "Oh, yes you bet I do." I asked him what was his favorite breakfast food at McDonalds (not even certain why I asked that question), and he replied with a sad tone, "Those hotcakes, you know the ones that come with that syrup. Man, are those good!" I immediately moved my purse to the other arm and handed him the McDonalds bag that had *his* breakfast in it. You would have thought the boy had been given a million dollars. He was shocked. He couldn't believe it and began chanting something like, "For real, ah no, for real, for real, this is for me?" His mom finally waited for us to catch up with her and she began telling the boy to say thank you to me. The boy was speechless. His heart was wide open. At that very instant in the heat of the summer's morning, the Holy Spirit made an opening for me to gently walk through to share God's love for His people. I looked over at the boy walking so proudly with those hotcakes on his arm and told him that Jesus loved him and that He never wants any of his children to go hungry. Do you think that opened up a place to share God's love? You bet it did. You see those hotcakes that I thought were mine were not; they belonged to the boy! I was just blessed to be the delivery girl! A brief, fleeting conversation no matter how short or long if anointed by the Holy Spirit can bring you such elation that your soul can literally feed thousands off of that one act of God's love for His people. And feed it did.

After I left the boy and his mom in the parking lot, my legs could have flown me to work that day as it brought me so much joy and peace knowing that the Lord's work was carried out that day and I was blessed to be a part of it. I sped up the stairs and called my friend, Deanna, and I immediately began speeding through the story of "Hotcakes and Jesus" so fast that she almost couldn't grasp it fully. As we talked, the Lord began using Deanna to point out that there was more to the story! Deanna, in her very warm, soothing way, pointed out that it was more than the boy who needed our prayers, it was his *mother* that needed them. She was on her way to face her son's day in court and her needs were great as well! "How could I have missed that?" I thought? Well, it was simple. "Hotcakes and Jesus" included not only me and the boy and his mom but it also included Deanna. She was the syrup on a very warm batch of mouth-watering hotcakes that the Lord blessed us with!

"Hotcakes and Jesus" is simple. It's about how God can take a plain old ordinary day and turn it into something miraculous- if we just ask. In our own strength we are nothing, but when God anoints our words and prepares the hearts of the listeners, His power begins to take over. *"I am the vine; you are the branches. If a man remains in me and I in him, he will bear much fruit; apart from me you can do nothing. John 15:5.* Imagine what would have happened if I would had just given the boy the hotcakes in my own strength. It would have been nothing, simply nothing exciting, just a simple act of kindness gone in a second. But not with the Holy Spirit directing my path. That act of kindness, anointed by God, became a monumental event. God allowed me to see how He poured out His love on that child so profoundly that the memory is etched so deeply into my mind, body, and spirit to this very day for what happened so long ago.

My conversation with God went something like this,

Thank you, Lord, for the hotcakes. I don't know what to say. Thank you doesn't seem adequate, but all I know is that you have used your mighty hand of power, love and guidance to fill me with a joy that is unexplainable, totally unexplainable. How mighty you are! How loving you are! And oh how you answer the simplest of prayers from the very smallest of your servants.

And with that, the ripple of blessings went on and on and on. For each time "Hotcakes and Jesus" replayed in my mind, I got blessed again and again. The desire to be used by God is not from our own strength; it comes from living our lives through Jesus. *And the gospel must be preached to all nations. Mark 13:10.* Loving others, proclaiming God's love, and performing acts of kindness can be supernaturally anointed by the hand of a powerful God who longs for you and for me to work for Him with every waking breath. We do serve a mighty God who can use the simplest of things for His glory. Just remember, it only took one small prayer of asking God to be used that day for Him to unlock His power, His love, and His blessings- and, of course, the anointing of Hotcakes and Jesus.

Chapter 11

Inside Out

Every ounce of my strength had been stripped away. I sat lifeless in front of my Master, my Savior, my everything, crying out with the only breath I had left in my tired, weakened body. Lord, Lord, help me! Without fail my Lord was there. It was His perfect love that took me out of the state of emotional ruin and set me free that nearly perfect Wednesday. But it wasn't until I was turned inside out through God's perfect spirit of love.

Anyone who has ever moved before and left behind friends, family, and all familiarities will know exactly how tiring life becomes when every single thing is brand new. No old faces, no familiar places, everything brand, spanking new, including life.

I sat in my husband's office chair (the one that makes you cry) so many times right after we moved and cried and cried. The story was the same. I couldn't find my fit. I couldn't nestle in. I couldn't find friendships. Tear after tear streamed down my face as my husband's ever-comforting hand lifted me up in prayer and love and understanding. The answer was right in front of me, and I didn't even see it.

I spent hours upon hours wondering why every time I went to something new, whether it was an event for the children or my husband, I just didn't fit in. And somehow I couldn't see the answer. Every time I attended a business, social, church-related or even just fun event, I couldn't find my fit. People passed me by as if I were invisible. Oh, there were formalities in that most would welcome me and ask my name, but that was it. It just stopped there. No other contact, no other conversation, nothing. It was an ever-present uncomfortableness that made me feel isolated, lonely, unwanted, unloved and, yes, even abandoned by God. I became withdrawn and saddened. I knew this was not my Savior's plan for me. He had made no mistake by moving my family, and He did want me to nestle into Godly relationships and make my life, my home where He had planted me. I began to grow weary from fighting the battle of trying to be "comfortable". But on one particular Wednesday after I attended a Ladies Bible Study meeting I left feeling a great need to talk to God. And talk we did. My conversation with God went something like this,

Father, Father, I am lonely, isolated and this doesn't feel like home. Why Father, why? I have tried to nestle in with these new faces, new places and it's just not working. Why, Father, why? I can't go on. I'm at the lowest place my tired, weak body can go. I call out to you for answers. WHAT AM I TO LEARN FROM THIS FATHER?

And without fail and with His infinite wisdom, loving spirit, and all-knowing, commanding voice I felt these words pour into my spirit,

It is a lesson of love. Pure love. The lesson is love, the love of humanity. You have not shown pure love to your fellowman. It is much more than just introductions and acquaintances; it is love. It is about loving your fellowman regardless of who he is, where he comes from or what he looks like. You, my child, must love your fellowman as if you have never loved before. It is by my hand that I commission you to love. Reach out. Love those who are lonely, that are not a part of the inside. When you show Christ's love to your fellowman you bring those into the circle of love that emanates from Christ's hand. It is my circle of love that can fill, edify, glorify, and, yes, bring those closer to you in abounding love. That is the lesson my child.

And with that, I found out why I was on the outside looking in at every meeting, every social event, everywhere we went everyday! You see, God is a God of love, and being polite and kind and serving others can only be glorified by the Lord if you reach out and show true Christ-like love for your brothers and sisters in Christ. I was there. I was polite. I was kind. But I stopped there. It's not that I wanted to stop at that point; it was that God needed to transform me into becoming more like Him and making me into His perfect image of love. I suffered tremendously by feeling like an outcast every time I went somewhere, but if it hadn't been for months and months of suffering, I would have never known how to go that step further and show pure love for others.

After that lesson was learned on that nearly perfect Wednesday, I began to see transformation after transformation in my relationships with others, in my daily interaction with people and my walk with the Lord. The Lord has revealed His true self to me in love and until you have had that perfect, complete transformation by God's own hand, you cannot know God's perfect love. You must be swallowed up in God's arms and He must command into you His perfect *love that is patient, kind, does not envy, does not boast, is not proud, is not rude, is not self-seeking, is not easily angered and keeps no record of wrongs. I Corinthians 13:4.*

This type of love cannot come from our own strength. It is truly from the power of the Lord. And the enemy will do anything possible from keeping you from attaining it. The enemy will put thoughts in our heads that we already love people or that we already know about loving others. After all you love your children in God's own love don't you? You see the enemy had told me over and over that God had already taught me how to love His people purely but it was simply not true. I had to reach out to God on that nearly perfect Wednesday and be turned inside out to receive this transformation by the Master's hand. It is only the one true and living God who can change us so dramatically to feel God's love. It is dramatic. It is life changing. It is an awakening in the soul. It is how the Savior desires us to love, from the very hand of God.

Do not conform any longer to the pattern of the world, but be transformed by the renewing of your mind. Then you will be able to test and approve what God's will is-his good, pleasing and perfect will. Romans 12:2. Renewing of the mind is the exact transformation I received from God so that I could love, as God desires me to love His people. If you cannot describe a supernatural, life-altering, thought-changing, perfect love that the scripture describes, then you might be where I was the day the Lord revealed deep inside of me His true and perfect love. My conversation with God went something like this,

Man,.......you rock!

Chapter 12

Waiting on Love

Feeling love is easy, right? But what happens when God calls us to love someone who doesn't want to be loved or someone who is difficult to love? Can God bring those persons together in a spirit of love? Why must we love those who hate us? Love, pure as gold does exist but it does not come from us, it comes from Jesus. Jesus is love, pure as gold. *Now that you have purified yourselves by obeying the truth so that you have sincere love for your brothers, love one another deeply, from the heart. I Peter 1: 22.* Learning from Jesus how to deeply love our brothers and sisters in Christ takes leaps of faith, steps of sincerity, and the walk of a giant. And that is just how I came to love someone deeply who didn't show me any love at all.

So many times I had tried to love this person I'll call Kate, but failure continued to discourage me. I knew that the Lord was calling me to love her, but it became so difficult. Kate wasn't easy to love. She was harsh, negative, angry, and opinionated and refused to admit when she was wrong. At my lowest point with Kate, I pleaded with God to just let me out of the relationship with her but God's answer kept pointing me back to I Peter 1:22, to love deeply. Sometimes I felt worn out at the sight of Kate. The enemy began attacking my thoughts so I Peter 1:22 could not be carried out. Satan was right in the middle of this relationship, which is what God wanted me to see in the first place. If there is a strife or indifference or hatred between you and a brother in Christ, God did not put it there, and He certainty doesn't want it to stay there! Our Master, our Creator desires us to love as Christ loved, pure as gold. Just recognizing that Kate was not the enemy and that Satan was the true enemy brought some relief, but that was only the beginning.

My relationship with Kate did not begin to seriously improve until I made some changes. I had to take a leap of faith and just allow God to direct me. My conversation with God went something like this,

Lord, I have tried over and over again to love Kate, but it always ends in strife, anger, and indifference. It's just not pleasant. Take this from me Lord. What is my next step? What should I do? How can this be solved?

A very loving and all knowing God had a brief conversation with me and it went something like this,

Pray for her. Pray for her night and day, without ceasing. That is the only step for you.

Knowing that prayer has dramatic results and that God never makes a mistake, I finally dug in and just prayed. I found myself praying for Kate in the car, in the kitchen, in the daytime and at night; my every thought was on her. I called out to the Lord so much for Kate that God began to reveal His truth to me. I didn't need to pray for restoration in my relationship with Kate, I simply needed to pray for Kate herself. God revealed to me that Kate had no love for herself and that the bitterness and anger in her personality was evidence of that truth. I prayed for Kate to have deliverance from things in her past that brought about the lack of love, lack of self esteem and the ongoing battle with herself. In the process, as God so uniquely designs, prayer melts the heart of those praying so dramatically that our differences seemed very insignificant. All I wanted was for Kate to be freed from her past. My heart had truly softened to Kate in every way. I no longer sought only my wants and my desires; I yearned only for what was best for Kate.

In God's time, Kate began to see herself as the true picture of love God intended her to be and, yes, even to this day, I am amazed and shocked that God used me to show Kate the true picture of herself. As we sat on the floor at Kate's house one Sunday afternoon, the Lord asked me to move aside and let Him work. Kate wasn't good at communicating, but she wrote well. The Lord used her ability to write to see in black and white the goodness inside of her as she listed topics under the heading, "I Am". The Lord used that list to show Kate all of the wonderful things inside of her and that gave us a starting point from which we talked and talked and talked. That day turned out to be the first of many conversations and many prayer sessions Kate and I had where we agreed to just let God be God and for Him to show us the way Jesus intended us to love, pure as gold.

God divinely reached out and showed me that love between two people cannot be pure from the Master unless Jesus is intimately woven into that relationship. *As the Father has loved me, so have I loved you. Now remain in my love. John 15: 9.* The Lord not only allowed a new friendship of love to develop between Kate and me, but a deeply, compassionate love in Jesus was interwoven as well. I Peter 1:22 at its finest.

Today, Kate occasionally still has battles with not feeling good about herself and sometimes it shows in her words toward me, but now I can look at her and see that God has not finished with Kate yet, and she is very much worth the wait!

Chapter 13

King Size Discipline

Disciplining our children is not one of those requirements we think about when we first learn that we are expecting a baby, but it's a fact of life. Discipline and children go hand-in-hand. What does God say about discipline? Are there consequences for not disciplining our children or disciplining our children in a spirit of anger? God holds near to Him all of His children, not just some of them, but all. We, as parents, are merely the vessel that God has chosen to care and tend for these children. I believe that God uniquely creates life and God also uniquely prepares a specific plan for correcting, guiding and centering our children God's way. Learning God's way of disciplining our children can be difficult and demanding but also life-altering and even sustaining for our children.

Allowing God to take firm hold of us as parents and teach us how to discipline the children He has entrusted to us can only please the heart of the Lord; I'm convinced of that. I know parents who have cried many tears over trying to find the right way to discipline their children, but God's way is simply the only way. God intimately knows each one of His children, and He alone knows what method of discipline is best for each individual child. *Teach me your way O'Lord and I will walk in your truth; give me an undivided heart, that I may fear your name. Psalm 86:11.* Tear that verse apart and you might just find your formula for disciplining your children God's way. For my husband and me that verse became our motto when it came to disciplining our children, but not before I turned to God in desperation after all that we had tried failed miserably.

Children can lose all sensitivity to each other's feelings, and teasing, taunting, and ridiculing can become a way of life. That's exactly what happened one quiet afternoon when both of my girls were running errands with me. As a mom I was ready to put an end to the arguing that the girls were engaging in, so I did. But I didn't do it with much love and very little compassion. In fact, it was done very harshly and I wasn't very slow to anger. God was listening. I was not.

We began to make our way to the car after a tough scolding, and both girls were quiet for the first time all afternoon. It was uncomfortable. We began trying to find our way to the car as I while squinted with half-opened eyes in the bright sunshine and carried my four-year old hugged tightly to my hip. My oldest daughter spotted the car and pointed us in the right direction. I started off the curve and so far so good. Nothing unusual. Then it happened! I got right beside the passenger side door and bam! It was sudden, instant and life altering! I went down. I just fell to my knees and onto the pavement! Out of nowhere I just fell with the baby on my hip, all of my weight and the baby's weight on my right knee. Wham, out on the pavement! No warning at all.

I tried to pick myself up. The baby wasn't hurt. I was still holding on to her with all of my strength while trying to lift myself up. My knee was all busted up, my arm was hurting and my right hand was beginning to swell. I managed to put the baby in her car seat and I looked over at my oldest daughter and just sat there. I struggled to pull my pain-ridden body into the car. I looked down and I just couldn't hold it together anymore. The tears started flowing, and my oldest daughter kept asking if I was okay. I couldn't even speak. I could feel a lesson coming, but I wasn't in any shape to listen very carefully. We all sat very still and quiet for what seemed like an eternity. My conversation with God went like this,

Lord, I know you are trying to tell me something; what is it?

I didn't hear from the Lord. My body was filled with the sin of disobedience and the only way I was going to find out what the lesson was, was to come before the holy throne of the Lord and ask for forgiveness. As I went to the Lord in prayer, I admitted my failure as a parent and asked God to teach me. God is so faithful to reveal to us when we have sinned against Him. And of course my sin came boldly before me. God was dealing with me in a big way. Miraculously, I didn't break my wrist or shatter my kneecap or even worse. The Lord protected me. I was simply bruised and a bit beaten from the fall, but just battered enough to stop and turn to my Father in prayer, which was the lesson itself.

When we as parents are at the very bottom and cannot find enough strength to go on guiding, instructing, and counseling our children God's way, we need to fall to our knees and get help. It may seem that all is lost, but the truth is God never gets to the point where He says, "You're right, this child is hopeless". As I desperately held on to my child when I fell to the concrete, my only concern was making sure she didn't get hurt. Nothing else mattered at that point, only that she didn't get hurt. God holds on to us in that same way. He never lets go of us, even when we don't discipline our children kindly or with love. He never lets go of us when we feel we have reached the bottom and there is no hope. God is still there and has all we need to not only survive but also thrive! God is a God of massive powers of hope and reconciliation. Turning to God for transformation with our words, our actions and our demeanor towards discipline can only lead us straight into the loving arms of God. God has shown me from a little fall on the concrete that He is still near when we as parents fail. He has shown me that He will hold on to us tightly when it seems impossible for us to get up. He has brought me into a place of prayer for my children where I have all of the power I need to manage. He has shown me with His massive arms of might and His tender loving touch that when we discipline our children; we need to do it with unconditional love over and over again, even for those children who repeatedly disobey just as the Psalmist describes the cycle of sin and sin again in Psalm 107. *But he lifted the needy out of their affliction and increased their families like flocks. Psalm 107:41.* God desires our increase. He desires us as parents to increase, increase in our knowledge, our courage, our strength, our determination and most of all, to increase in Him. God doesn't desire that any of us as parents be in bondage to a disobedient child or give up hope on any of our children. He alone has the answer when there seems to be none.

When I turned to my heavenly Father on the day of that fall, I was in need of a lesson of king size proportion on disciplining God's way. God wanted more for me. God wanted more for my children, each of them. He got my attention, and I became still. The stillness of the fall allowed me to focus on Him, His ways, and the error of my own way. It's sad to say but true. I had disciplined my older daughter in anger not in love. My words were not pleasing to the Lord when I spoke in anger and I knew it. *In your anger, do not sin. Ephesians 4:26a. My conversation with God went something like this,*

Lord, you alone have the power to give me guidance with these kids. I cannot discipline without you. It is only with your strength and your wisdom that I can manage this task of discipline. Show me your way. Teach me to be more patient. Show me how to discipline one child and then the other, individually. Help me to be fair, consistent, and help me simply to be obedient to you with these kids. I can be strengthened through you Lord! I can walk away from disciplining these children with confidence, strength, and honor through you Lord, only you!

With His wonderful face of love God reached out and burned a message deep into my heart that day in order to keep me in His love and in His way. Being in God's love and God's way meant disciplining my child supernaturally, totally and completely God's way, pure love without even a hint of anger. It meant choosing my words very carefully to build her up and not tear her down. It meant loving her as God, the Father, loves her. Pure love. Unconditional love. Corrective love and a sure measure of discipline grasped firmly together with God's guidance was the only formula I needed to carry out God's will, discipline my children, and maintain a strong sense of emotional health for all of us.

God is a loving God and full of compassion for His children. But He requires a certain level of discipline from us as parents, and if we do not heed God's warning, then the consequences may be dire for not only us, but for our children as well.

In 2 Samuel 18 we see King David mourning the death of his child. *The king was shaken. He went up to the room over the gateway and wept. As he went, he said: "O my son Absalom! My son, my son Absalom! If only I had died instead of you – O Absalom, my son, my son! 2 Samuel 18: 33.* I simply cannot think of anything worse than a parent mourning the loss of a child, but King David's mourning may have been even deeper than that over the loss of a child. We see a King with a very tender heart for Absalom and as a result, he did not discipline Absalom. Imagine how he must have felt looking back realizing his mistake. Even King David felt the woes of parenting. Whether you are tender hearted like King David and find discipline difficult to carry out, or you are simply in need of God's loving touch and supreme guidance, He is waiting to speak to you. Disciplining our children cannot be done without supreme counsel. He guides. He corrects. He loves. He listens. He forgives. He rewards, and He protects.

As parents, we have several choices when our children are in need of discipline, and the outcomes for each choice may be dramatic and life altering. If we allow God to penetrate our hearts with His method of disciplining our children, we cannot fail. We will be taking instruction from the very creator of the heavens and the earth which will bring forth a king size proportion of glory and honor to the Father! *For it is not those who hear the law who are righteous in God's sight, but it is those who obey the law who will be declared righteous. Romans 2:13.*

As I buried my face into God's hands and cried tears of joy, I had truly found that disciplining our children God's way was nothing more than a way for the very words of God to be poured out on them by the Father. What love!

Our Conversations
with God

On Purifying & Refining

Chapter 14

The Blonde, the Brunette and the Red Head

G od is the Master of details, the details that concern you and the details that concern me. It's difficult for us to imagine, but God knows every detail about each of us, our personalities, our likes, our dislikes, and our past, present and future. He alone is God. *Indeed, the very hairs of your head are all numbered. Don't be afraid; you are worth more than many sparrows. Luke 12:7.* In my mind I simply cannot imagine how God knows the very hairs on our heads but His word tells us so, and that's enough for me. But God is so much more than a being that takes count of the hairs on our heads; God wants the very best for us, and He will go to extreme measures to see that we get that, His very best. For me God jumped right in the middle of something I never would have imagined, my hair color, and began orchestrating a huge event that would ultimately bring about His divine will.

Changing hairdressers can sometimes be experimental, but God reached out with His hand of patience and mercy after I visited quite a few hairdressers to teach me how to submit to His will and His will alone.

It began like any other typical hair appointment with consultation, color and styling. But as I looked in the mirror at the final product I saw a bright blonde color that somehow just didn't fit. I tried to pretend it was okay and ignore the strands of blonde hanging around my face, but they persisted in bothering me all of the way home. My daughter didn't have any problem announcing to me that my hair was very, very blonde. I still didn't say anything but pretended all of the way home that the color was fine.

I walked into my husband's office trying to be optimistic and sat down slumped over in his very sturdy chair that pointed straight at him and said nothing. He knew I didn't like the color of my hair. I still remained silent. My husband, being the comforter that he is, continued to reassure me that it wasn't so bad. It didn't work. The blonde color had to go. Blonde was somehow natural on me but this was different; it just didn't fit. In fact it was so unsettling that the entire life crept out of my body. But somehow I knew I wasn't upset because of the color of my hair; it was deeper than that. There was a certain element that was drawing me to pray about the color of my hair. I did just that, and the Lord spoke to me deep within my heart. My conversation with God went something like this,

Lord, I know you can see me, and I know you knew I would be unhappy with this blonde hair even before I left that place. Right? So, what am I to do?

In the deepest and innermost chambers of my heart, I felt a wonderful, magnificent God reach out to me, and His conversation with me went something like this,

Be yourself. Simply be yourself and not the person you are pretending to be.

I said nothing but I knew exactly what the Lord meant, and it spoke volumes to me. My conversation with God went something like this,

Lord, give me strength to be myself and to be happy with who I am inside and out. I just need strength and guidance. Will you help me do that?

After spending some time in prayer just seeking what God was really trying to tell me, I could feel that somehow I was getting ready to make some internal changes that would affect the external part of my body, my hair. I knew what I had to do, but I also had to break the news to my husband.

I opened the door of my husband's office and plopped down in the same chair that a few minutes before had held my slumped over body. This time it was different. I was taller, bolder and beginning to step into life with a new color. But the bad news was I had to break this to my husband who had a long-standing request concerning my hair – keep it blonde! Yikes! I had a mini-conversation with God real quick, and it went something like this,

Lord, I'm not sure I can go through with this. I'll need you to speak!

I looked my husband straight in the eye and told him I needed to change the blonde hair. He wasn't surprised. As I waited for a response from David, I got none. So I dug in and quietly asked for courage and told my husband that I was not coming back blonde. He suddenly turned his eyes to me and asked if I was sure about that. I didn't know how to respond. I just told him it was what I needed to do.

I left his office still in a state of unrest. I simply could not get peace about my hair color and I didn't know why. *The way of the Lord is a refuge for the righteous, but it is the ruin of those who do evil. Proverbs 10: 29.* Turning to the Lord and seeking Him was my only answer in solving the unrest. As I sought answers from God, I could feel the problem was much deeper than hair color, and that God was planning the beginning of a more fruitful relationship that did not include resentment, anger, bitterness, or conditional love. And, yes, hair color was the root of the issue. God has such infinite love for His children that He was providing a refuge for us that neither one of us could see.

As I sought God on my end, I knew that David was the other player in this event who needed also to seek God, so I waited. Minutes seemed like hours, and hours, seemed like days, as time seemed to have stopped. Finally David came to me with a saddened face and eyes of pain after seeking the Lord in prayer, and I knew all was not well. I assumed if I weren't blonde, then David wouldn't love me as much. Satan is very clever that way to take illogical assumptions and make them seem realistic. I knew God was calling me at the time to get rid of the blonde hair so I was hesitant to comply because of that ever-nagging assumption in the back of my mind. I once heard a Pastor say that if there is an area of obedience that God has made known to you, just watch out! Satan will always make a way for the disobedience to occur. That was so true. Satan had planted the idea in my head to just leave my hair color alone because blonde really was best for me regardless of what God was calling me to do- an easy out for me to be disobedient to the Lord simply by listening to that ever present thought.

My husband and I joined hands with heavy hearts, and our conversation with God went something like this,

Lord, we love you and we want our thoughts to be held together by nothing but you Lord Jesus. Speak deep into our hearts and reveal to us what is the true issue behind Susan's hair color and help us to have ears to hear and eyes to see your will.

The seconds ticked away in complete silence. Then out of nowhere my husband began professing his guilt, guilt that he didn't even know he had. He had shame for creating this image in his mind of what I should look like and not loving me truly unconditionally.

He continued to confess solemnly to the Lord; His conversation with God went something like this,

Lord, I am so sorry. I just want you to change my heart so that I am more accepting. Cleanse me and help me focus on you and not color! Sew this marriage together as never before and you decide on Susan's hair color, and if it's never blonde again, then that's okay. I just want to be pleasing to you and love my wife the way you want me to love her. And most of all Father, forgive me for making Susan try so hard to be something she's not. I love her deeply, this you know and we ask that you bring good out of the deception we both have endured. In your precious Son's name I pray. Amen.

Words cannot express what I felt at that moment. All of those years of starvation diets, bleaching my hair, and numerous other things I did to try to please my husband and look the way he wanted me to were finally over. Just like that. Finished. I was free to be me. And at that point I had a profound thought, I didn't even know what I really looked like!

There are many things that can confuse us and make us act or behave in ways that only God can explain. This was clearly one of those things. It's important to understand that coloring your hair blonde in itself is not bad. Experimenting with hair color can be exciting, fun and uplifting if it's done in the right manner. Clearly I did not do that in the right manner as I used my blonde hair to pretend to be something that I wasn't, and God revealed that to me very clearly. *In the same way, I tell you, there is rejoicing in the presence of the angels of God over one sinner who repents. Luke 15: 10.*

At this point, the only thing I knew to do was to try and glorify God with my hair color. I prayed for wisdom. Off I went for another salon visit praying all of the way and in walks the brunette.

The salon visit started off simple. I wanted to get rid of the blonde and go to some shade of brown close to my natural color. After painting an unknown color on my head and then washing it out, followed by much conditioning and heat drying, out popped the new color. The towel poised ever so delicately on my head came off and WOW! I was a brunette! Ah! It's very dark! I'm still breathing but not sure about this. The stylist reassured me how wonderful this "shade of dark brown" was on me. I still wasn't sure. My conversation with God went something like this:

God, here I am. I did it. But somehow, I don't think this is it. Oh boy, what do I do now?

I knew I was headed for home at that very moment. So off I went. After a few weeks, the brunette color began to fade and red tints began to creep over my hair. I didn't know why at the time, but I became unsettled again about the color. Although I didn't realize it at the time, my very dark hair fading to a shade of red was simply God preparing me for His will to be revealed. I waited for my designated time to get color again and in walks the red head!

Visit number three started off simple, and a noon appointment turned into a marathon hair appointment. It began with the consultation. The orders this time – it's too dark. I would like it a lighter shade of brown. Simple, right? Maybe not. The stylist explained in all of that technical mumbo jumbo that I had semi-permanent color on my hair in some sections and permanent color on other sections and my natural color at the roots. She lost me around the semi-permanent explanation. Still not knowing why I felt that way, my only request was this – make sure it gets rid of the red tint.

So I went to the color chair for what was supposed to turn out a light shade of brown. After manipulation after manipulation, the towel was finally pressed down on my head and the verdict was in. As I pulled the towel off my head, my body went into shock! I couldn't move. I wasn't even breathing I think. My dark hair was not dark anymore; it was a heavy red with brown on the bottom! The stylist told me not to panic. It was too late for that! It was dramatically red and even as she dried it partially, my face looked as if I had a 102-degree fever as my scalp lay bare and exposed through the new color. I thought, ah, Lord help me! My conversation with God went something like this,

Lord, I'm trying to get this color thing right, but this red I've not planned on.

The Lord was so good to have spoken deep in my heart. His conversation with me went something like this,

It is well. It is well. It is well.

I sunk in the chair and waited for the stylist to offer a fix for the "goof-up". She quickly said if I could stay she would redo my roots and make me darker to get the top to match the bottom. Now remember, this is not the same stylist from color # 1 to color # 2 or color # 3. The hairstylist was not the problem. God was still in control. I agreed to have it fixed. I went back to the color chair again.

They began painting an unknown color on my hair once again. I'm shampooed for the 4th time, and the towel is again placed on my hair. This time I'm convinced it's to cover up the color! I didn't even want to look. The stylist pulled the towel off again and wam! The red hit her in the face, as my hair was aglow! I didn't know what to say. She didn't know what to say. My conversation with God went something like this,

Lord, I'm here trying to be obedient to the call to be myself but all of these other colors keep popping up on my hair. This is no coincidence. What's up, what are trying to teach me?

The Lord said nothing. But I felt a spirit of conviction that ran deep within me. It was me! I had not submitted to the Lord's will totally, and as long as I, Susan, could pick my hair color, I would agree, but if the Lord chose a color not in my options, I wasn't game for it. Well, red was it. I knew in the back of my mind that my husband didn't want me to have red hair. He had made that clear to me much earlier. At that time I simply gave in and I knew in my heart that the Lord would simply have to work on my husband at that point because I was going home a red head!

The Lord gave me a peace that overwhelmed my spirit, and suddenly the red color on my hair was not even an issue. I was at peace and knew God was going to accomplish something through this color "issue", and I was anxious to find out what exactly He was up to.

The stylist continued to express sorrowful comments and continued to tell me that she wanted me to be happy. After several more shampoos, I was off, but this time with the dark shade of brown I walked in with and a heavy red tint that the Lord would use to His glory.

I phoned my husband and tried to explain, and he chuckled, but I could tell he was wanting to see just how red it was and how he was going to handle that. Well, the Lord began working on him instantly.

After about 48 hours of the heavy red tint on my hair, my

husband and I were heavy in prayer asking for answers, as my husband was clearly not treating me the same. Suddenly his spirit was deeply convicted him of unforgiveness and anger. Those feelings clearly not of God, were a result of resentment he had many years ago against a person who had, you guessed it, red hair! If you think God doesn't know your deepest and innermost thoughts even before you, this is clearly proof of it! God has full knowledge of things completely unknown to us and desires us to acknowledge and release those things that weigh us down so that he can ultimately make us whole and renewed again.

We did that in prayer, and David's conversation with God ended something like this,

......thank you Lord for bringing up things that I didn't even know existed. You have my mind, thoughts, feelings, actions, and most of all my wife. I thank you for using Susan's red hair to bring out those ungodly feelings, and I ask that you bless her for being used to bring these things out in me. I am yours, and now you can use me fully in whatever manner you see fit. Boy, Lord, are you good! We are amazed at how you can take a simple thing like hair color and bring glory to your name. We love you, Lord, and can't wait to see what color is going to be on Susan's hair next......

After going from blonde to brunette to red haired, I realized how much focus I had placed on my hair color and how little that pleased God. For me, being blonde meant being super, king-sized, self-absorbed, and focusing on pleasing my husband instead of God! *I am the true vine, and my Father is the gardener. He cuts off every branch in me that bears no fruit, while every branch that does bear fruit he prunes so that it will be even more fruitful. John 15:1-2.* That was one branch that desperately needed to be whacked off! When I was a brunette, I still had not died to self, and I found myself desperately trying to control God. It didn't work!!! When I was a redhead, I wasn't willing to put David's desires under God's. How sad! But God reached out and gave me so much more than I had before through that very lengthy series of battles with my hair color. The Lord used each color to reveal to me my true inner self and my willingness to allow God to lead. I felt reconciliation with God as never before!

And as for my hair color today, I know that whatever color rests upon my head, from blonde to brunette to red, that within each color there will be something gained, something lost, and something yet to be found.

Chapter 15

Small, Weak and Needy

Are spiritual giants huge in stature, bold in nature, and chocked full of confidence? Are they gifted in speaking, teaching, and preaching? Do they have confidence and charisma, or are they small, weak, and needy? God found His way so deep into my heart and buried the answers to those questions so powerfully into my spirit and my mind that I was forever transformed. The thought that God couldn't use the small, simple, needy and the weak disappeared, and there arose a very determined and ever so small fish in the sea that longs only to swim with God each day. I wish that were the end of the story, but the real truth is that the enemy wants to chew you up and spit you out until you have nothing left to offer. The enemy wants you to believe that you are insignificant and cannot possibly be used by God. If you have ever felt even just a twinge of this deep inside of your thoughts, then ask God for the truth. I did. He spoke. I listened. But swimming with God each day might not be what you are expecting. It sure wasn't for me.

Ministries come in all different shapes, forms and sizes. They may not all be visible for the world to see and some are so visible you can't even see the top! Sometimes the ministries that God provides us take us out into the world, and other times we stay right at home. I've seen a teenager take several pieces of brightly colored chalk and use his artistic abilities to teach other kids about Christ all over the United States, and I've seen my very own mother-in-law bake literally thousands of loaves of bread to take to those sick, lonely, or suffering for years and years. God wants to use each of us in our own way to care for those hurting or perhaps to care for our very own families.

God put me at home with my small children for a season and my main job was to grow them, feed them, nourish them, encourage them, care for them, and fulfill God's purposes in their lives. He gave me a home ministry. Oftentimes the Lord gives us a ministry, but our eyes are blind to the very blessings He puts before us. Other times ministries pop up when least expected. That is exactly what happened when the Lord swept me up and told me to write.

I had no idea that a book ministry was coming, although my husband had told me quite some time before, that he felt I had a book ministry. My idea of a book ministry at that time was simply going to a Christian bookstore and allowing the Holy Spirit to lead me into purchasing the right book for the right person. I could literally spend hours exploring and finding nuggets of God's wisdom all over those stores. God was preparing me for His work on each trip I spent book shopping. The wisdom of the Lord is profound!

I began writing and feeling very small, weak, and, yes, very needy as a writer when I realized that the enemy was pounding my thoughts and telling me how useless it was to write and that it was simply a waste of time. And on one solemn day I entered our church library filled with hundreds of books, and I sat down to have a conversation with God. It went something like this,

Lord, as I look over the mountain of books in this place, I feel so totally overwhelmed. Do you see that this calling to write makes me feel so unqualified? Why, Lord, why are you calling me to write? I just can't understand it. There are so many others who are gifted to do this; why Lord, why am I being called to write? Help me, Lord, to understand.

And with that prayer the Lord deeply, deeply placed His hand of comfort around my shoulder and softly whispered to me the purpose for the book ministry. I knew from that moment forward that I would not be like any other writer on the bookshelf and that I didn't have to compete with other writers because God had a specific purpose for me. I no longer had to live up to being the biggest fish in the sea. God told me to write, regardless of how small I felt, and that was all I needed to do was to follow that command and let God breathe life into that ministry.

As an extraordinary lover and teacher of God's Holy word, my sweet sister in Christ, Nita Tin says, "He never takes you into any "place" where His grace cannot keep you! He never asks you to speak, but that He hasn't already laid up His words in readiness for you to share." That profound thought has God's power and determination embedded in each word, and regardless of how small you may feel or how large the task God is calling you to embark upon, it is not our own strength or ingenuity that will bring that ministry to fruition. It is simply the power of an Almighty God giving us every single thing we need to accomplish His will, from the tiny, little pencils needed all the way to the deliverance of a life-changing speech prepared for nations!

Realizing that we are not the ones accomplishing any of these great feats of success on our own and that it is truly our Lord who gives us words, wisdom, and divine guidance for the things He calls us to do was a pivotal point in my removing Satan's stronghold over me in the area of being small, weak and needy. And as that stronghold was broken down, I turned to our Heavenly Father for strength and guidance. The Lord graciously remade my thoughts into His truth, and purity and I became bright, bold, and confident as the enemy's power was diminished in Jesus' name.

Fishes

*Father, I'm swimming in this big ocean that
you've put me in and I know not where to turn.*

*I turn to the left and I see blue.
I turn to the right and I see blue
Help me Father to turn only to you!!*

The fishes are fast. They are sharp.
They are plentiful and they are ripe.

You Father God made me this fish and you
will set my fin on tightly time and time again!!!

And set my fin on tightly time and time again is exactly what the Lord did each time He called me into an area of service or ministry that I didn't know how to begin. Being a spiritual giant in Jesus' name doesn't mean you have to be the best or the biggest or the strongest. God will give you the sea in which you are to swim. For some of us it might be the ocean; it might just be a small stream trickling down the mountain. But one thing is clear, when God calls us to be a light before nations, He gives us every single thing we need to fulfill His purposes including time, confidence, energy, determination, helpers, and a sure peace that can only come from a God who knows our name and even the hairs upon our head. Spiritual giants often have tiny footsteps and small voices led by the hand of Christ. It just takes a willing spirit who says "yes" even when it seems impossible, unreal, and so far out of reach. God does use the small, the weak, and the very, very needy!

Chapter 16

Puzzle of Life

Finishing a tiny puzzle with each piece put together and fitting firmly in its designated place creates such a feeling of accomplishment and vision. Seeing the entire picture brings us comfort and assurance. It leaves no room for doubt or uncertainty. But what if the pieces of the "puzzle of life" cannot be seen? What if they never seem never to logically fit together? How can we, the promised children of a merciful and loving God, overcome the desire to see the entire puzzle? Does a person stricken with cancer not want to know if they will live or die from this disease? Does a person unemployed not want to know when he will be employed again and provide for his family? Does a person who suffers from depression not want to know if the depression will end or if there ever be joy again? It's human nature to want to know the answers to the questions that we are faced with in life, but it's a God thing when we can look our circumstances straight in the face and not be concerned with seeing the entire puzzle neatly fitting together.

The crowd joined in the attack against Paul and Silas, and the magistrates ordered them to be stripped and beaten. After they had been severely flogged, they were thrown into prison, and the jailer was commanded to guard them carefully. Upon receiving such orders, he put them in the inner cell and their feet in stocks. About midnight Paul and Silas were praying and singing hymns to God, and the other prisoners were listening to them. Acts 16: 22-25. Do you think Paul was concerned about the "puzzle of life" when he was thrown into jail after being severely beaten or was he content just to sit tight and allow God's plan to masterfully unfold right in front of his eyes? Oh to have the contentment of Paul! Oh to have contentment when our "puzzle of life" doesn't make any sense at all.

My dear friend Darlene Crabtree looks back over a lengthy battle with breast cancer and sees how God's masterful hand was so good to her during the deepest struggle of her life. The puzzle piece called "breast cancer" came upon her, and while there were questions of life and death, she clung to the promises in God's word. That puzzle piece was certainly unexpected, but God's plan was set. Whenever we receive a puzzle piece that doesn't make sense to us, we must first realize that we are human and we cannot understand all that life holds. I have heard my friend Diann Sivley say, "God didn't give me Leukemia, but He saw me through it." We can be assured in the midst of our most fierce battle that God is present and His blessings are forthcoming and that we are not always privy to why things happen as they do in our lives.

As Darlene Crabtree struggled to survive breast cancer, she has told me time and time again about much more her life means to her now, and how much more patient she has become with her husband and how much God has taught her to trust no matter the situation. Darlene has suffered many setbacks and times of uncertainty, but through it all her faith has grown and her love for her Lord and Savior has been nourished, thickened, and melted together into God's will for the good of the whole body of Christ. God's blessings were clearly in sight as we, the onlookers, saw a transformation of her own might!

God wants each of us to become spiritually, physically and emotionally strengthened, not just those of us who are suffering from illness or disease. He wants all of us! I have found that God's way of preparing us for His works of service often comes unexpectedly and when it makes the least sense to our intellect, but ultimately the entire body of Christ is strengthened and unified for the good of all. *It was he who gave some to be apostles, some to be prophets, some to be evangelists, and some to be pastors and teach-*

ers, to prepare God's people for works of service, so that the body of Christ may be built up until we all reach unity in the faith and in the knowledge of the Son of God and become mature, attaining to the whole measure of the fullness of Christ. Ephesians 4: 11-13.

How passionate would we be about going about God's work in a specific ministry if we had not experienced the same hurts and same pains of those we minister to? If God called you into a hospital visitation ministry, and you had not been exposed to sickness, illness or hospitalization, would you just go and make the visits and check your "to-do" list off, or would you deeply and compassionately pray for those you visit and continue to minister to them beyond the hospital bed? We need to be refined and taught by a wonderful Master and Savior who seeks only for good and desires us to be taught and prepared for the work of His service. For Darlene, going through the trauma of breast cancer and the complications of that illness refined in her a more sensitive spirit to those hurting and suffering. Her ability to see pain and suffering has been newly manifested by God's merciful hand and tender arms of love all around her wonderful body. Darlene's puzzle piece called breast cancer, illogical as it may have seemed in the beginning, brought about a new ministry for Darlene and good for the entire body of Christ.

Sometimes our puzzle pieces fly at us so fast that we feel like we are just swatting at them and trying to catch the next piece and to clearly fit it firmly into place so that we can see our entire "puzzle of life." There may be threats of downsizing at work or a marriage wavering in uncertainty or parents that are becoming frail, weak and closer to death. But regardless of the circumstance, you can know that God can be trusted, and that He alone is your Provider, Redeemer, Healer, Master, and Savior. Taking those puzzle pieces that bring us fear and doubt and uncertainty and embracing them into our arms of trust for the Master's plan is oh so pleasing to the Father. Trusting God in times of illness, disease, disobedient children, difficult relationships, financial problems, or even a nation in uncertainty will produce a faith greater than you know now. It will please the heart of the Lord and draw you closer to the Father in all things.

The Heart of the Lord

The heart of the Lord is for His people.
His people who long to worship and adore Him.

The heart of the Lord cries out for His
people in prayer and supplication.

The heart of the Lord is mighty and longs for
His people to draw near to him.

May your heart yearn to know the heart of the Lord!

Yearning to know the heart of the Lord embraces those things in life that are uncertain and complicated and truly unknown. As servants of a truly wonderful God and Savior, we can be assured that God will take care of His own. *Cast your cares upon the Lord and He will sustain you; he will never let the righteous fall. Psalm 55:22.* That one sweet Psalm has enough energy in it to push a locomotive around the world indefinitely with one single push! God promises us that we can endure uncertainty and undergo adversity in our lives. Oftentimes that adversity brings us purity. It brings us a cleaner and more refined spirit. When God purifies our lives, He brings His power over us in such a commanding way that oftentimes we feel we are being purified to a fine powder when in reality there are still many clumps yet to be sifted through. My own "clumpiness" has brought me into times of uncertainty and times when there was no clarity for what God was doing or allowing in my life. It was in that time and that time alone that I find myself desperately seeking God in order to know the truth. As I turned to my heavenly Father for answers, my conversation with God went something like this,

Lord, I know that you alone have the answers to all that life holds for me. I don't ask for all of the answers; I just ask for your truth to become clear to me. You knew my circumstances even before they

arose. My future is uncertain. My health is unsure. My thoughts are filled with doubt. My longing is to please you. My desire is to be sick as long as you need me to be sick. Give me enough faith to maintain your will and carry me through the times of pain and fatigue and uplift me during the times of doubt and fear. Take this puzzle piece that I can't even see the name on yet and use it to your glory. Whenever you see fit to show me the name of this puzzle piece that is causing this pain and sickness, I will not turn my face downward, I will arise and be strong only by your hand. You are awesome! You are mighty! You are my healer! You are my Savior! You are simply all I need to see. The future is clear, crisp, and full of hope as your hand is all I need to see. Take me, hold me and clearly show me your way.

Perhaps that prayer should have included a measure of patience in it, as the unknown puzzle piece that was causing so much uncertainty in my life became a reality some seven months later with no date of departure indicated! When pieces of our life seem long and unending and totally illogical, you can rest assured that a God of love and purity is at close watch over us, bending, forming, shaping, and molding us quaintly into His firmness, wholeness, and ultimately, His righteousness. It is that righteousness that we desire that allows our perseverance. *Perseverance must finish its work so that you may be mature and complete, not lacking anything. James 1: 4.*

The "puzzles of life" that we all desperately want to see hanging prominently on the wall in perfect order secured by a frame of certainty are often best kept in the Father's hands until His divine time arrives. God is so full of surprises and full of miracles that if we could look at our own "puzzle of life" full and complete and completely in sight, we could match the pain to gain, the despair to repair and the challenge to triumph. The real test is not being able to put the "puzzle of life" together, the real test is being able to leave pieces of our lives unanswered and unsolved and knowing that God's blessings are closer than we think in all things certain and uncertain.

Chapter 17

Me on the Outside, You on the Inside

Gazing into a mirror at the age of 15, 25, 45, 65 or even 85 can bring a whole range of ideas and concepts of beauty that range from innocence and purity to luster, glamour, and radiance to even wisdom. What is beauty? The New American Webster Dictionary defines beauty as: 1) the quality of an object or thought that arouses admiration, approval, or pleasure, 2) a particular trait, grace, or charm that pleases. Does God see beauty when He looks at you or at me? What do you see when you look at yourself? Is it the truest form of beauty?

God created the heavens and the earth without blemish. God is the truest source of beauty. He alone is beauty. Nothing can compare to His beauty. God's grace and majesty radiate a beauty our eyes have not seen! God is beauty and we are His creations, also full of beauty. God in His mighty splendor creates beauty. Grasping God's beauty with eyes full of the world will make the view of ourselves distorted, twisted and incomplete. But taking firm hold of God's hand and asking Him to reveal His truth about your personal beauty will be like walking hand-in-hand with the Master in the cool of the evening.

Mirror images can often distort our view of who we really are and what we are truly made of. Some of us may look in the mirror and see imperfection or hopelessness and others may look into the mirror and just accept what they see. But when God looks at us, He sees so much more! When God looks at us, He sees what we cannot. *The King is enthralled by your beauty; honor him, for he is your Lord. Psalm 45:11.* It took a four-year old and curiosity with a camera for me to learn a powerful lesson on beauty inside and out. Our youngest daughter loves to take pictures. On one cool fall afternoon, she began snapping shots of me. As I looked at the photos, I saw imperfections and flaws in myself. It was as if the life had been taken out of me. I was greatly saddened and knew I needed some time alone with the Father. I called out to the Lord and my conversation with God went something like this,

Father, you know how I'm feeling already, and I know it's wrong, but somehow I just can't shake this feeling. As I look at myself, I no longer see youth, vibrancy, or luster. Please help me to see your truth.

Spending time alone with the Father is simply priceless. He guides, He instructs, and He gives nuggets of His wisdom. His conversation with me went something like this,

My child, when I look at you I see something quite different. I see beauty. True beauty. I see deeper than what is on the outside, I see the entire face. I see the face of a woman who cried when her daughter got on the school bus for the first day of school; I see a mom who just spent time riding scooters with her little one; I see a wife who gives her love freely to her husband; I see a servant who wiped away tears of someone else's child who was hurting. I see you. You are beauty. Your life is beauty to me. You are beautiful to me completely. If you dig deep, dig deep inside beyond the surface you will see the beauty that I see, that is only perfected in me.

As I sat still and quiet before the Lord, I knew that the enemy had been hard at work twisting, deceiving, and blinding me from the truth, God's truth. Beauty comes from Jesus. Living a life full of Jesus with every ounce of strength we've got produces a beauty that cannot compare with any other. We can use all of the cosmetics we can find, have the most magnificent hairstyle, wear prominent jewelry and the most exquisite clothing, but the real source of beauty begins with Christ living deep down in our hearts and wearing our beauty through Him. *One thing I ask of the Lord that is what I seek: that I may dwell in the house of the Lord all the days of my life, to gaze upon the beauty of the Lord and to seek him in his temple. Psalm 27:4.* Gazing upon the beauty of the Lord does not mean looking at His face and seeing attractive facial features; it means knowing God intimately from within. God's word tells us that we are made in His likeness, so our beauty doesn't wholly consist of our facial features either; it is living in Christ that gives us our beauty! What freedom God's truth brings. God with His loving arms of guidance, swept me up and revealed His truth about my beauty and choked out Satan's tool of deception that had been used against me my whole life.

Knowing God's truth about beauty and applying God's truth about beauty are not synonymous. We can say it all day long, but until we truly feel it deep down in our hearts, we cannot grasp God's true beauty. God knows what we really feel about our own beauty; we cannot fool Him. He is all knowing! For me, I could not release God's truth on my life until I asked Him to help me. I had no power to do that on my own and truly mean it. I could say my beauty was more than just my outward appearance, but I didn't really mean it. God knew that. By simply praying one quiet afternoon, His power was unlocked on my life and allowed me to see the depth of beauty through the Master of Beauty Himself.

God loves us so much that He desires us to live in His perfection and not our own. Looking into a mirror, at any age, reveals me on the outside and Jesus on the inside. There is nothing more loving, sustaining, and comforting than knowing that I don't have to depend on what is on the outside to bring me joy and peace, and that God looks upon me and upon you with such pleasure. *The Lord is in his holy temple, the Lord is on his heavenly throne. He observes the sons of men; his eyes examine them. Psalm 11:4.* God does see His people. He observes them. Beauty is deeper than we can see with our own eyes; it begins with God and ends with God. That is seeing me on the outside and Him on the inside.

Chapter 18

A Visit from God

Imagine you are nestled in a soft, cushy, warm, comfortable bed asleep with the covers tucked all around you engulfing your whole body when suddenly you are awakened. Instantly you are awake and it is as if God himself has just tapped his finger on your shoulder and awakened you. You are not groggy or drowsy but completely awake and upright. Your ears are waiting to hear something but you're not sure what. You sit very still and silence fills the room. The presence of the Lord is near, and He has come to talk to you. You cannot see Him but you know that His presence is in your very room. You still cannot move. You cannot turn to the left or to the right. Your mind is sharp, your hands are still, and you begin to get anxious when suddenly a reverent fear overcomes your whole body and you cannot move a muscle in your body. It is stifling, overwhelming, and totally consuming; God has commanded your full attention. But what if God commanded your full attention in other ways? What if God allowed you to suffer physically or contract a terrible sickness or disease? Could we be as faithful as the Old Testament character Job during that type of visit from God? *If only my anguish could be weighed and all my misery be placed on the scales! It would surely outweigh the sand of the seas-no wonder my words have been impetuous. Job 6:2. Yet if I speak, my pain is not relieved; and if I refrain, it does not go away. Job 16:6.*

Pain in its most intense form can be easily understood or not understood at all. We can all empathize with a woman in labor desperately trying to birth a baby into the world. Her pain brings forth the sweetest of blessings, but what happens when the pain we suffer doesn't bring forth something tangible for us to see? Do we remain faithful? Do we curse God? Do we give in to depression or anxiety and allow the enemy a foothold over our mind and our thoughts? It's very easy to be on the outside looking in, answering all of those questions, but until God reaches out His hand of mercy and touches *your* shoulder to awaken you with a trial of pain and suffering, you might be hard pressed to even continue living. I found myself at that point after years and years of being afforded a very healthy body.

The Lord chose to awaken me spiritually by allowing my body to go through some of the toughest trials of physical suffering I've ever endured. It began so quietly that I never even saw it coming. Little by little I began to notice that something was wrong with my body. I tired easily and became extremely fatigued after minimal work. That condition was coupled with the pain of recurrent infections that made a normal days routine impossible. I suddenly found myself wondering if this condition was going to improve, stay the same or get worse. The weeks lingered into months, and the pain intensified to the point of my being homebound for rest, quietness and care. Doctor after doctor could not explain the symptoms or diagnose the problem. My conversation with God went something like this,

Lord, you see the condition my body is in. I know this has not happened out of a freak coincidence and I know you are in the middle of this. Teach me whatever you need to teach me and get me out of this thing quick!

At that second God burned a message deep into my spirit that brought about new light to a dim situation. His conversation with me went something like this,

It is well my child. It is well. No doctor will be able to diagnose

your condition until my divine time is appointed. Rest well and know that your sufferings will produce something greater for you, and you shall be blessed. I shall raise you from your bed, and you shall be afforded healing in my time. It is only my time. Trust and remain faithful.

God was allowing a new level of faithfulness to be deeply buried into my heart that I could not see, feel, or touch. I cried out for answers. *O'Lord, the God who saves me, day and night I cry out before you. May my prayer come before you; turn your ear to my cry. Psalm 88:1-2.* And God was faithful to answer. During that time of sickness and suffering in my life, the Lord was so good to give me nuggets of wisdom as I picked up my pen. I buried those insights into paper to read, reread and read again. As I sat one day listening to God, this is what I felt deep in my heart as His conversation with me went something like this,

My child, physical sufferings will make you strong. They will make you commit to prayer, and they will make you appreciate the absence of them. Physical sufferings will grow your faith and put your focus on me despite the circumstances around you. It will make you yearn to read my word, and they will help you to lose all pride and ask for help. These sufferings you are experiencing will bring hope for your future. Your body, mind, and spirit will unite for the same purpose, healing. Your sufferings today will produce the mind of Christ and produce obedience for your future. You are not suffering in vain and you must have enough faith to suffer as long as I will. I have not forgotten you, and you are walking in my light right this very minute. Rest in me. Abide in me.

God's promises are powerful, and they can never be taken away. God had promised me that good would come from the pain and suffering that was striking my body and with that I focused on Him and allowed time to be my friend and God's will to be my own. *Not only so, but we also rejoice in our sufferings, because we know that suffering produces perseverance, perseverance, character; and character, hope. And hope does not disappoint us, because God has poured out his love into our hearts by the Holy Spirit, whom he has given us. Romans 5: 3-5.*

As that time of waiting and wondering about my health disappeared, the Lord brought forth beauty from the ashes and fulfilled each and every promise made to me. *The end of the matter is better than it's beginning. Ecclesiastes 7:8a.* The pain that my body endured was for a specific reason, and as I look back I can see no other possible way God could have softened me, burdened me, and instilled in me the value of loving and caring for those who are sick and suffering with every ounce of strength I could muster. It was God's way of purifying and refining and giving to me more than I had before; yes, that visit from God commanded my attention and gave me the full attention of a truly loving and ever-present God!

Our Conversations with God

On Prayer

Chapter 19

A Fog of Sorts

Picture yourself driving on a very familiar road that suddenly becomes thickened with a sheet of fog. Your visibility is choked off. You slow your car to a creeping pace. You sit up straight, stretch your neck out to see better, but your vision is greatly impaired. Nothing is on your mind except the fog. Fear begins to race through your veins, and your heart quickens. You have become critically aware of all that is around you. You yearn only for the second, not for the minute ahead or the hour ahead but only that second. Your attention is consumed with the fog and your ability to see what's ahead. You cannot see. The thickening has consumed your eyes. The fog is immersing deep into your mind, and your hands are clutching the steering wheel for life. You remain persistent and continue driving forward, not backwards, not pulled over to the side but straight forward. The seconds seem like hours and the heavy covering of fog begins to lift. You have a slight bit of visibility. You sit back somewhat in your seat, but you are still not comfortable. You continue driving but still very, very slowly and methodically. You can now see the road as the fog is lifting a bit higher. The grip on the steering wheel begins to soften. You become a bit more relaxed. Your breathing is almost normal when God steps out in front of the car and asks you a powerful question. You slam on the brakes and listen with ears of passion. God looks deep into your heart and asks you if you felt His love, His presence, and His power during the fog. You know the answer and your face turns downward. God draws His massive arms of compassion around you, His dear child, and holds your face softly in His hand and tells you, "I will protect you in the deepest and darkest of times of your life! I am God!"

How reassuring that even when our darkest days arise we have hope. God has promised to be there for us through the loss of a job, the pain of an addiction, the sufferings of cancer, or our ongoing struggles with sin. There is nothing that can keep us from the love of God! *Neither height nor depth, nor anything else in all creation, will be able to separate us from the Love of God that is in Christ Jesus our Lord. Romans 8:39.*

I was so blessed in having met a young lady I'll call Emma. Emma was in her early twenties and had a thriving personality. She brightened up the room by just bouncing in with her sweetness. She was full of energy and had a charming demeanor. I had gotten to know Emma through business and had never seen anything but her girlish charm and bright smile. But one day Emma was quite different. Her spark for life was gone. Her demeanor crashed to the ground. The life was completely drained out of her body. She began to talk. I'm convinced God had divinely allowed us to meet on that day.

As Emma sat in front of me, I saw all of the charm ooze out of her weakened body. She began sharing with me the reason for her pain. She confessed to working a night job just so she didn't have to spend much time sleeping. Sleeping was her enemy because at night she saw vivid dreams of what was attacking her life. Her pain worsened as she spoke, I could barely contain my hurt for her. I desperately needed God to intervene. He did.

Emma sat lifeless as her words gushed out about the cause of her pain. She couldn't even find words to tell me what was really bothering her, but she did manage to say that she had very, very big sin and that God could never forgive her because it was so bad! I prayed for God's words to fill my mouth as I moved aside. The Lord wanted Emma to know that she was so loved by Him and that He knew of her sin and was standing there at the door waiting for her to come to Him to ask for forgiveness and receive His love.

Emma cried tears of regret, sorrow, and pain and said that she had done something so awful that she couldn't even ask for forgiveness. I leaned in and took her hand and told her that God was waiting for her and that all she had to do was release it to Him and He would forgive her. She held her head up and looked at me in amazement. She told me that she was filthy, and she couldn't imagine me holding her hand. I gripped her hand tighter and just looked into her eyes while the Lord softly opened her heart. We both cried and remained still, neither of us speaking. As the sorrow remained deep within Emma's heart, she couldn't make the leap of prayer she needed to make. Her thoughts were so filled with her sin and guilt she couldn't take my hand and pray. I was grieved. As we continued to talk for nearly two hours, Emma was in need of some time to think. I had the horrendous task of letting her go not knowing if she was going down to the bank of the Mississippi River to do business with Satan or to reconcile with God. I had a very short conversation with God and it went something like this,

Lord, what do I do now?

I knew in my spirit as the words to the Lord burst out of me what I had to do. But God is so willing to give us confirmation when we ask. His conversation with me went something like this,

Entrust her to my care.

As we parted, I felt a sense of failure and disappointment, and I didn't even know if I would ever see Emma again. I painfully got in my car and left. My every thought was on Emma all night long. I desperately wanted to call her, but I knew God was at work and I just needed to trust Him. But that was an awful lot of trust, so I found myself deep in prayer for Emma's life. The next day proved that God is larger than life and He alone is trustworthy. *Those who know your name will trust in you, for you, Lord have never forsaken those who seek you. Psalm 9:10.*

I awoke the next day to a bunch of sprawling, long stemmed red roses awaiting me without any note. Finally after almost a whole day, I heard from Emma. It seems her conversation with God on the bank of the Mississippi River went something like this,

Father, forgive me. I am a terrible sinner. Save me from a life in hell. Make me over again I pray.

I stood there in utter amazement at how one simple prayer turned Emma's life around and set her on the road paved by the very hands of God himself. That is the ultimate prayer! For Emma her years of being in a fog of sorts ended and allowed her to walk by faith that God would forgive her and make her over again. Her vivacious personality and zest for life newly enriched by the Holy Spirit brought me more energy and determination no matter how desperate life seemed.

A Fog of Choice

Father, this place I cannot see,
Your hand I cannot see.
Your will I surely cannot discern.

Help me O'Lord; help me!
I need vision, direction and clarity.
Bring your light into being for me to see your
plan and yes, the future as you hold.

The road my child you cannot see.
It is the fog thickening with the faith you desire.

As your faith stretches, the fog impairs your vision
and oh how glorious this is, only of the Father.

Allow your eyes to only see the very edge of today
and allow the fog to overcome, engulf and surround,
your hand as placed carefully upon the Master's land.

The fog is about to go.
Your faith will now show.
You have endured the sight of the unknown and
your future is surely shown.

Embrace the fog.
Seize the thick covering of God's hand and nurture
your soul with careful plans, not of man.

The fog of choice brings comfort and peace as the
Master, Savior and Great Redeemer of all so eloquently plans!

For me my fog was not knowing what would happen to Emma when we parted that day. God was there. A fog that is massive and penetrating can only be entrusted to the Master's hand. As for the roses, Emma would never take credit for them, but I knew they were from her. The roses lay today crisped and preserved, and each time I look at that bouquet of wilted red roses I think of Emma and the way God preserved her life never to be thickened by the fog again.

Chapter 20

24/7

Trying to connect to someone can be as easy as picking up the phone and calling or as simple as just sending an e-mail once in a while, but how difficult is it to connect to God and stay connected to God? There is one method, one measure, one source of eternal connection to God this is swifter than the fastest Internet connection known to man and as sure as the sun rising every single morning, and that is prayer. Prayer. Prayer. Prayer. As children of God, we have a never-ending source of power, a vast expanse of wisdom, an immeasurable supply of knowledge, and a tremendous amount of God-given treasure when we connect to God in prayer.

Whenever we ask Christ into our heart we become one with the Spirit, and we have access to God the Father, Jesus, the Son, and the Spirit of God all in unison, tied together, just awaiting our connection. We are powerless without that connection. That connection is prayer. When we offer our prayers to God, we connect, intertwine, and interlock to a magnificent God who gives hope when there is none. But what happens when we can't feel that connection to God in our lives?

For some of us our lives fill with things that we don't identify specifically as trouble and it becomes increasingly difficult to connect to God with those things in our lives. And to top that, we just can't understand why we feel distant from God. Most of us want to stop and turn to the next chapter at this point because this simply doesn't apply to us, right? Well, you can tell Satan right here and now that you will gain knowledge and you will hear from God and that you reject his lies in the name of Jesus. We will all endure times of trouble, despair, and hurt. Ecclesiastes says, *There is a time for everything and a season for every activity under heaven: a time to be born and a time to die, a time to plant and a time to uproot, a time to kill and a time to heal, a time to tear down and a time to build, a time to weep and a time to laugh, a time to mourn and a time to dance. Eccl 3:1-4.*

One of the tools Satan uses is the tool of deception. Satan has a very clever way of deceiving us by convincing us that our lives are perfectly comfortable, and that everything is going well but the truth may be far from that. Do you feel lonely? Are you frequently unsure about the future? Do you feel exhausted day after day? Do you have children that honor you? Do your friends bring honor to the Lord? Do you own any possessions that you may put above God? Do you harbor unforgiveness against someone who may have hurt you? Satan will tell you that none of those things are problems for you; while those things may truly be real burdens, heavy and weighted on your heart. The Holy Spirit is the only one who will speak truth into our ears and paint a realistic picture of our lives-real, honest, and from the mouth of God. In order to see the truth, we must ask for the truth! *Then you will know the truth, and the truth will set you free. John 8: 32.* Ask him. Listen and be still.

By the world's measuring stick, we may have all we are "supposed" to have. We might be sitting comfortably in our warm, cozy homes. But the truth is, only God can make a house a home. Only God can turn unforgiveness or the coldness of a relationship into love as deep as human emotion can allow and embrace to become natural. God desires us to live in peace and know Him fully. We cannot come into the presence of the Lord and receive all He has for us if we have resentment, bitterness, anger, hatred, jealousy, strife, or anything that chokes the spirit of God out of our lives.

One of the most difficult times my husband and I experienced was the feeling of helplessness when a couple that we knew experienced such turmoil in her lives. Our conversation with God went something like this,

Lord, they know you and love you. But they doesn't take time for each other. They cry out for love, yet the other is blinded. They live together, but they do not truly talk to each other. They praise you, but they cannot feel each other in their relationship. Bring about peace, love, and softness in this marriage. Breathe life into this relationship. Bind the enemy is Jesus' name. Let there be no busyness in their schedules to keep them apart day and night. Allow them time to spend with you, Lord God. Bring them closer together, and we ask for a miracle in Jesus' name.

As hard as that was just to pray and do nothing else, it was exactly what we did. In the deepest and most sensitive part of my heart, I believe that those prayers were probably the most important and the most valuable thing we could have given that couple. Don't let anyone tell you differently! The enemy will creep in and tell you that your prayers are meaningless and that they simply cannot help. That is a lie! God wants you to know the truth about prayer. Prayer is our very own intimacy with a truly loving God who yearns to hear from us day and night, 24/7. I've not known any other relationship to have total and full access anytime day or night like we have with our Lord and Savior. Our faith never takes a vacation from prayer, it is ever persistent, it is always on the job and never turns away from another assignment. The realities of a broken relationship, a home without peace, a spirit of unforgiveness, a spirit of strife with our children, or our children's friends, or a spirit of discontent will always provide us opportunities to pray.

In fact, it is oftentimes those prayers offered up for others in need that actually sustain life, give continued support, and thrust us into the future. One of those times that literally thrust me into the future was when a lady whom I just barely knew after moving hundreds of miles away from family and friends whispered softly to me one day that she had been praying for me and my family. That one utterance of God's love for me gave me enough energy, stamina, and determination to dig in and move forward. The prayers of Susie Westbrook offered up in God's love and God's care delivered by a truly faithful servant made for one encouraged, one determined, and one truly strengthened child of God. I am a living and breathing example of the strengthening power prayer really has. Even when we don't realize that we are in need of strength, the Lord uses the prayer of others to provide us refreshment, and energy and give us more than we expected.

As children of God we are always in need, in need of the Father. There are times when our spirits are so weak that we feel we can't even pray. Listen up. There is no such time! None! When you are at your weakest, God is standing there ready to strengthen you in an instant. The enemy wants to believe that you are too weak to pray but that is a lie! If the enemy can make you believe that then he's got you right where he wants you – disconnected from God. Crying out to the Lord in prayer when we are weak is familiar, familiar even to the psalmist. The psalmist cries out to the Lord and says *O'Lord, the God who saves me, day and night I cry out before you; turn your ear to my cry. For my soul is full of trouble and my life draws near to the grave. Psalm 88:1-3.* Our strengthening is found in God. It cannot be found in reading magazines or books, talking on the phone, going for a drive, or eating our favorite dessert. I have personally gone from a state of severe fatigue, exhaustion, depression, with a totally lifeless body to a refreshed, perky, go-get-em attitude by simply praying in a matter of minutes. When you call on the name of Jesus, He shows up! Prayer cannot be underestimated. It is powerful, invoking, unleashing, sensitive, persuasive, commanding, soothing, loving, giving and, yes, very pleasing to God.

Prayer takes you places. Prayer changes things. Prayer gives you the ability to communicate with God deeply and personally. Prayer is thought provoking. Prayer invokes God's power on our lives and who doesn't need that? But prayer is up to you. It's up to me. Don't get caught in the trap of the mopping the floor prayer! The mopping the floor prayer is similar to how you begin when you mop the floor. You fill the bucket up with water and stop at the same line each time. You begin mopping in the same spot and you end your mopping methodically, routinely, and without a doubt in the same spot. You tip toe out to begin all over again the next time.

Prayer is so much more than mopping the floor! Sure we want to be thorough, but why start in the same spot? Could it be that when we begin and end with the same words that our heart really isn't sheered open and that our minds are just methodically working? I shudder to think of the times my mind has wandered during prayer when my heart really wasn't purely open and desperately seeking God. Prayer is so much more than planning what we are going to say in advance. Let the moment guide you. Let your heart speak loudly and boldly to God. Your words are important to God; all of them offered to Him in prayer are precious. Can you remember every single word of the very first prayer you had with God? Probably not, but God knows! *And pray in the Spirit on all occasions with all kinds of prayers and requests. Ephesians 6:18a.* There are all kinds of prayers - loud ones, desperate ones, gentle and soft-spoken ones, boisterous ones, elated ones, but most of all, sincere prayers done with the purest of hearts.

The purest of hearts also knows that prayer is a fine example of faith. In the book of James we see The Prayer of Faith. *Is any one of you in trouble? He should pray. Is anyone happy? Let him sing songs of praise. Is any one of you sick? He should call the elders of the church to pray over him and anoint him with oil in the name of the Lord. And the prayer offered in faith will make the sick person well; the Lord will raise him up. If he has sinned, he will be forgiven. Therefore confess your sins to each other and pray for each other so that you may be healed. The prayer of a righteous man is powerful and effective. James 5:13-16.*

Prayer is a full circle. Picture a complete and perfectly rounded circle with God in the very center. There are points high, let's say north, and points low call those South, and points in the middle, call those East and West. Wherever we are in life, whether low in a valley of depression or high on the mountain of contentment or somewhere in the middle, the Lord stands in the very center of the circle awaiting our prayer. We eventually make the full circle and begin all over again. It's not a surprise to the Lord at which point you are sitting on your personal circle of life today. He's there and is waiting to hear from you regardless of wherever you are on high or low. Prayer from your heart spoken to the Lord brings peace and great soothing as the Psalmist so eloquently wrote in Psalm 116. *I love the Lord, for he heard my voice he heard my cry for mercy. Because he turned his ear to me, I will call on him as long as I live. The cords of death entangled me, the anguish of the grave came upon me; I was overcome by trouble and sorrow. Then I called on the name of the Lord "O, Lord, save me!" The Lord is gracious and righteous; our God is full of compassion. The Lord protects the simple hearted; when I was in great need; he saved me. Psalm 116:1-6*

Prayer, Said Right

*Prayer, said right is so precious in God's sight.
It praises the King; it humbles the proud,
It takes us away from the crowd.
It draws us near when turbulent times produce fear.*

*Prayer said right cries out day and night.
It pleads to the Lord and King to be free from the pain you see.*

It is so soft, so sweet and so meek, prayer done right is so precious in God's sight.

*Prayer said right offers the true light in the full circle of God's might.
Offer your prayer right and begin the circle of God's love and it's never ending site!!!!*

Offering your prayers to the Lord reveals the true condition of the heart, so unselfish, so loving, so caring, so giving, and so in tune with the Holy Spirit. Being able to pray from the Spirit of the Lord can give others encouragement to make it and not give up in hopeless situations or at least what appear hopeless. On a very desperate day, I picked up the phone and called my dear friend, Jane Phemister and simply asked for prayer. We talked about how God was getting ready to provide but we just needed something to hold us over.

Jane's "From Here to There" prayer, as she called it, gave me enough stamina to do just that, make it until God's divine time when He saw fit to relieve burdens weighing heavy on our hearts. God is always in control of every situation weighing us down, but He uses prayer warriors to get us "From Here to There." Prayer is the very bandage that holds us together and keeps us firmly in God's care.

Prayer also has a way of creating time. Imagine a couple desperately seeking each other's love and companionship, but the intense pressures of schedules, children, and responsibilities crowd out any chance of that happening. In walks God for a little encouragement, chunks of love and answers to real big prayers!

Week after week after week, my husband and I had been trying to spend time together alone and something would always interrupt the plan, the date, the schedule. We had gotten to the point of just giving up when a friend suggested that we make a date and stick to it no matter what. She was right. We began to pray for the date, the time and the place. We had a plan. We prayed very "loud" prayers to God for the enemy to be bound from preventing this date from happening. I'm convinced the enemy was the great interrupter of our time together anyway. Everything was set, the date was on, and it was about 24 hours until the time.

A friend was scheduled to come over and chat with us the evening before our date. This person didn't know of the difficulties we were having getting time alone, but the Lord knew. Michelle Eskine is a great friend of God and her passion is seeking God, the Father. Her heart is so in tune with the Holy Spirit. There are some people in life that when they speak you know the Lord is divinely giving them guidance; Michelle is one of those persons. We were so blessed for having some time with Michelle and her son Baron that evening. The time went by so quickly, and before we knew it, it was time for Michelle to leave. Michelle being the servant she is for the Lord, began to pray for us before they left, and her conversation with God went something like this,

...............*Lord, you know the hearts of David and Susan. I ask that you bless their marriage. Take them and give them time to just love on each other, get their nourishment and use the time for sharing, talking, and building up their love...............*

After Michelle finished praying, I wanted to fall over in complete amazement at how the Holy Spirit had spoken to her about what we needed so clearly. She had no idea we were having problems spending time together or enriching our marriage, yet the Holy Spirit directed her to pray for that specifically. She didn't know we were scheduled to go out and eat the next night and spend time alone for our first date in ages. Michelle didn't even know what it meant or why she was praying for that, she just felt it, prayed it and let God be God! Michelle Eskine is so big in God's presence, and she is simply just a woman praying. Prayer is so huge, and what an example of a commitment to prayer done fervently, passionately, considerately, lovingly, and in God's spirit.

Michelle couldn't have given us a better gift than her prayers that night, and she continues to offer her prayers up in honesty, love and endurance. One such test of endurance was her oldest son. As Michelle's oldest son was being called up to go to Afghanistan in the most turbulent of times, her words were very soft and were very few but they truly spoke volumes to me. Michelle told me one night that her son was getting ready to leave to report to duty and that *her only job was just to pray for him.* That's it, just prayer. So calm, so peaceful, so caring, loving and, yes, so committed. And as you might guess, Michelle is a finely crafted example of how God can create the words, give you the time, and use you to provide support and encouragement through prayer, prayer done 24/7.

.

Chapter 21

Unchain the Door!

Children are so innocent, and when they talk about their feelings, their feelings are pure, strong and sincere all in the same breath. If you ever want a deeply honest answer to something, just ask a child. The innocence of children has the power to strike at our hearts when they speak, share, and even pray. Nothing pleases the heart of the Lord more than the innocence of a child praying; I'm convinced of that. Children pray little prayers with big meaning. They pray from their deepest desires and hold nothing back. Children are clear about what they want and they never doubt that it's going to happen. They pray and then just release it. Oh, how that must please the heart of the Lord....*Let the little children come to me and do not hinder them, for the kingdom of God belongs to such as these. I tell you the truth, anyone who will not receive the kingdom of God like a little child will never enter it. And he took the children in his arms, put his hands on them and blessed them. Mark 10:15-16.*

Picture a God that is busily hearing the call of each of His people and then out cries a small, simple, tiny, little voice, and God quiets the very lilies of the field to hear that voice. It's so important to Him when our children pray. They pull their deepest feelings outward and give them to the very hand of the Lord when they pray. The Lord receives them with such compassion, compassion that no man knows. His love for His children is so expansive we cannot humanly hold it in our hands. But God's hands most certainly hold it. He holds the love for His children so closely that when one of His children prays He draws them closer to Him in love, kindness, sincerity and His awesome compassion.

On one particular night when putting our youngest one to bed, she decided that she needed to pray for her sister. She knew her sister was having a hard time and needed some help. Alex's tiny little conversation with God went something like this,

Dear Jesus, um, please help my sissy. Amen, Lord.

That was it. No fluff. No beating around the bush. No extras, just plain, simple and to the point. She knew the Lord knew what that meant, and that all she needed to say was just help her. Her tiny little prayer told God that she trusted Him to do whatever He needed to do to help her sister. She had total confidence that it would happen, and she rolled over and went into a sound sleep. She didn't need to stay up and worry, nor did she need to call her friends to tell them what was going on. She just told God what was on her mind, and it was totally and fully released into His care. Can you imagine how gently and tenderly our Lord and Savior received that tiny little request? In my mind I see our Lord putting out His massive hands so gently and catching her words so carefully and looking at each word she used so delicately and tenderly not to miss one single part. I see our Lord placing her tiny little request deep into His own heart and feeling her sincerity, her generosity and her expectations in one single swelling of emotion, love.

As we place our requests into the Father's hands, do we entrust Him or do we dwell on what we think should be done? Are we confident that He will take care of our requests or do we doubt and worry and then doubt some more? When children pray, they pray as scripture tells us to pray-in faith, honesty and sincerity. *But when he asks, he must believe and not doubt, because he who doubts is like a wave of the sea, blown and tossed by the wind. James 1:6.*

Children also strike a sense of humility in others when they pray as well. I remember one Wednesday night at a Youth Prayer

Meeting when a group of middle schoolers began sharing prayer requests. God spoke to my heart very deeply when one 6th. Grader began to speak; I'll call her Jennifer. Jennifer raised her hand very confidently and began to speak. The room was silenced. Jennifer very boldly told the Youth Pastor that she needed prayer because she hadn't been eating healthy foods and that she had developed some other problems as a result of her eating habits. She went on to explain in detail those problems and asked for the group to pray for her. Do you think Jennifer had any pride when she shared her problems with a large group of her peers? How many of us would be willing to stand up before our peers and admit we had a problem with our eating habits and then explain the details and then simply ask for prayer? Jennifer stated the facts, released her problem and didn't look back. How many of us would be able to tell all and then walk around in total confidence with our peers? It is simply the power of Jesus in our children that humble their spirits and allow them to walk comfortably without the presence of pride.

God loves us so much that He offers our very own children as walking, living, breathing examples of true humility. I can only shudder at the times I have prayed and held back my true feelings to a Lord and Savior who already knew I was holding back. Coming before the Father and ridding ourselves of any smidgen of sin can only open the door to our Lord and Savior that much wider.

Imagine a conversation between a loving God on one side of the door and His child on the other side with the door only opened wide enough for the chain to be kept properly in place. Take the chain off the door! Be bold with the Father. Ask the Father to remove the slightest bit of envy, jealousy, hatred, gluttony or any other evil that exists so deeply in our hearts and in our minds. He alone can do that for you. He alone will hear you. He is God. Now imagine God, the Father, on one side of the door and His child on the other side of the door and the door begins to open wider and wider and wider until the door is completely opened and there is no sight of the door at all! That is the power of God's presence in our lives and the absence of all sin. Now we are truly in the presence of the Lord! The door is supernaturally unchained and we are in the massive arms of our Savior.

As our children teach us how to approach the Savior with

honesty, sincerity, and true humility, they have no chain on their door. They just begin speaking, and the door opens wide for them. But facing hurts, disappointments, rejection, negative relations, and impurities can create a little pocket of sin deep inside our hearts that we may not even know exists. We can easily see surface sin, such as anger, that can keep us from the arms of God, but digging out sin that is deeply embedded into our hearts isn't as easy. It may take the arms of a God-directed Counselor or a Pastor to help us remove anything that keeps us from truly developing an intimate relationship with Jesus Christ. There is simply nothing more precious in life than getting on your knees and praying as the little children do with absolutely no hindrances in our way to keep us from the love that God is desperately trying to give us. I'm convinced that God does not like chained doors in our hearts!

Our Conversations with God

On the Enemy

Chapter 22

Time Capsule

Putting something away for safekeeping to be later opened again may be what comes to mind when we think of a time capsule. But what is a spiritual time capsule? Do we make spiritual capsules without even knowing it? What if the things we have tucked away in our capsules come back again and again and again? Can we ever be rid of those burdens, pains, hurts, past mistakes, or sins that have already been forgiven and cast out of our lives? Lean in and listen to this - Absolutely! Our Father God is so merciful to us that He forgives us and cleanses us completely- not partially- never to be remembered again. There are no spiritual time capsules with God where our sin or past hurts are locked away and forgiven and healed only to resurface and hit us in the face again. That is the work of Satan trying to bring feelings of unworthiness, uselessness, regret, sorrow, pain, and a future without hope. When God cleanses, He cleanses completely and so lovingly hands us a fresh, new start as only He can. *Let us draw near to God with a sincere heart in full assurance of faith, having our hearts sprinkled to cleanse us from a guilty conscience and having our bodies washed with pure water. Hebrews 10: 22.*

The enemy can take firm hold of us and keep us in his grips with our past mistakes and failures. It is as if the door to the time capsule keeps getting opened back up and all of our dirty sins and painful hurts keep surfacing again. Feelings of hopelessness and despair quickly arise and we find ourselves falling away from God just as the enemy has planned. The enemy knows we cannot be used fully by God if we are depressed, full of sorrow, and lacking zeal for God's work.

My dear friend, Jane Phemister, once told me that when her husband passed away she knew she had to draw nearer to God, pick herself up and remove the depression because she couldn't bring glory to God being depressed. How mighty! In order to receive God's full blessings Jane knew she needed to give God the glory regardless of the magnitude of her own pain.

Giving God the glory is so much more appealing than fighting the enemy, but the truth is, if that ole' time capsule keeps getting opened up, how can we bring God glory anyway? We can't. But we can remove the enemy's presence in our lives; it just takes some work! As my husband and I look back, we can see how the enemy worked massive chunks of destruction in our lives, and the more the enemy threw at us, the more it sent us to the Father in prayer. Our conversation with God went something like this,

Father, the enemy is pounding us into the ground. We cannot even feel your presence in our lives; we are in a war zone. Please help us, Father, we cry out to you for your love, your mercy and your help.

Days turned into weeks, and our strength began to falter; the enemy was pulling us down, and spiritually we were falling behind. The Lord was present but we could not see His full and masterful plan to give us aid against the enemy until one day when our dear pastor and friend shared some of his childhood pains with us. He told us how the enemy had a foothold over his life and how he overcame it with Christ. The pastor shared with us that during his upbringing his father told him quite frequently that he would never amount to anything, and those thoughts stuck with him throughout his life. Satan used those haunting thoughts of not amounting to anything to discourage, disillusion, and ruin this man's self confidence, self-worth, and plans for his future. But Jesus gave him a way to be free of those bobbing capsules of unworthiness. It took a measure of getting tough with the enemy and using God's Holy Word to remove the enemy's presence in his life. For David and me, it was a lesson in fighting the enemy 101.

We soon learned that God's word has all, all of the power to overcome the enemy! It is the mightiest tool we can have in our spiritual tool belt against the enemy's attacks. God's armor is one of the simplest weapons God gives us to fight the enemy, and we found ourselves not even using it! We soon learned that we couldn't survive one single day without putting on the full armor of God. *Finally, be strong in the Lord and in his mighty power. Put on the full armor of God so that you can take your stand against the devil's schemes. Ephesians 6:10-11.*

We used God's word to rebuke Satan and brought down thoughts of unforgiveness, shame, and guilt, and reminders of a sinful past and removed Satan from our lives! *I have given you the authority to overcome all of the power of the enemy. Luke 10:19. With God we will gain the victory, he will trample down our enemies. Psalm 108:13.*

The enemy wants nothing more than to condemn us for our past and render us useless, depressed, angry, agitated and distant from God. I have found that the enemy won't just surface our own sins against us, but he will surface a hurt from the past that someone else may have caused us. Those hurts may have been buried in the capsule long ago, but Satan has resurfaced the capsule in hopes that we will open it up and look inside and dig up the past. *The thief comes only to steal and kill and destroy; I have come that they may have life, and have it to the full. John 10:10.* God knows of our struggles with the enemy and wants us to be forever freed. God wants that time capsule sealed shut and propelled deep, deep into the ocean's bottom never to bob up again.

Getting tough with the enemy and reclaiming our position in Christ was the only way David and I were freed from the grips of the enemy. Whenever those capsules of long ago resurfaced, we knew they were of the enemy and we spoke God's word in the face of the enemy strongly and boldly, "I am a child of God! I am forever free from condemnation!" For me, Satan used my past fears to bring doubt about my future and create division between my husband and me. I claimed *II Timothy 1:7 For God did not give us a spirit of timidity, but a spirit of power, love and of self-discipline.* But remember, your capsule has to be completely airtight! Having an airtight capsule means that you have no holes to allow Satan to re-enter your mind, your thoughts, or your actions. Becoming airtight is a God thing. If you have had to dig deep in your heart to forgive someone or to put your own transgressions behind you, then you may be prone to a leak of unforgiveness, anger, guilt, hatred, bitterness, envy, jealousy, sexual immorality, lust, or mistrust. No matter what is causing the hole in the capsule God is bigger than the source of the leak. There is no level of forgiveness that is too big for God. There is no level of hatred that God cannot change into pure love. He is God. Asking God's help to plug the leak in our capsule is simply the only way to obtain freedom from the enemy.

God in His loving splendor wanted so much more for David and me than just surviving the enemy's attacks. He wanted us to obtain freedom in Jesus name! He gave us tools of spiritual guidance and words of wisdom from a concerned pastor; He gave us scripture verses to use against the enemy and the full armor of God with a bonus of lasting relief from condemnation. David and I walked away from that battle against the enemy knowing that our minds, bodies, and our spirits had been strengthened, enlightened, renewed, encouraged, and loved by both the very Word of God and His loyal servant, Rev. Ron Tyndall, a man of deep spiritual truths and Godly wisdom, who was very, very giving of his time.

Time capsules and safekeeping are best left in the Father's hand as sin and our past in the hands of the enemy can only be managed and put to rest by the massive and powerful hands of God in Jesus' name. Make no mistake about it; the victory has already been won! *Therefore, there is now no condemnation for those who are in Christ Jesus, because through Christ Jesus the law of the spirit of life set me free from the law of sin and death. Romans 8:1-2.*

Chapter 23

Masking the Mountain

What comes to your mind when you think of a mask? Is it something frightening or something playful? The New American Webster Dictionary defines a mask as 1) a covering for the face, worn for disguise, protection, etc. 2) anything that conceals, a pretense. A mask can be used for many purposes and worn at anytime. When is the last time you wore a mask? Are you wearing a mask right now? Chances are, you answered no to wearing a mask right now, but was that really true? Could you possibly be wearing a mask right now that is invisible to the world but apparent to God?

Wearing a mask that is invisible to the world is as easy as masking our images so that the truth doesn't come and make us look weak or needy. Maybe we don't want others to know that we have hurts in our lives, so we smile and pretend everything is fine. But is it? We mask our conversations when asked how our day went. We mask our feelings when we talk about our marriage. We mask our emotions when we talk about an unanswered prayer. Sometimes our masks become so thick that we cannot even be seen anymore. Our true identity remains hidden, sealed, and restricted.

God loves us so much that He wants every single burden that we are carrying, masking, and hiding deep inside of our hearts to be revealed, carried out in prayer, and fully turned over to Him so that He can reign as Lord and Savior over us each breath we take. *The spirit himself testifies with our spirit that we are God's children. Now if we are children, then we are heirs - heirs of God and coheirs with Christ, if indeed we share in his sufferings in order that we may also share in his glory. Romans 8: 16-17.* We are God's children, so how can a Father not want to help His very own creations? I am convinced God does not want us to mask our feelings and our hurts deep within us in order to survive. There is a better way! It is Jesus. It is Jesus. It is Jesus. What a mighty counselor we have in Him! Picture yourself entering this office. This is not any ordinary office; this is the office of the Almighty Counselor. As you enter the office, you see Jesus sitting comfortably behind the desk with a nameplate that simply says, "Jesus" sitting inconspicuously on the desktop. There are no initials behind the name indicating status, rank, or authority from which He is qualified to teach those who come to Him. It is simply Jesus. As you sit down, the room feels smaller than what you would have imagined, but there is a sense of warmth and genuine concern for you and you alone. As you glance over the desk, you look at the wall and see a frame hung quietly beside the door. You would automatically assume that a prominent degree or counseling certification would be enclosed in the frame, but it is not. It is simply a picture of a large, broad, deep, heavy, wooden cross. It reminds you that Jesus knows every pain you are suffering. He knows the weight of your sorrow, and He knows the anguish of your heart. As you begin talking, you kick your shoes off, find a nice comfortable spot in the chair while Jesus listens and consoles. You realize that there are no pains, past or present or future, that cannot be handled in that room, and while you may have entered with your mask on, you might be surprised at what you will look like when you leave.

Picture another room. This one is different from the first one described. This room is filled with chattering. It is also filled with many people rather than just two but Jesus' presence is known and truly felt by all, just like the first room. I was privileged one night to be a part of a group of young to middle-aged men and women from all walks of life. As I sat down, I listened carefully as each one of them asked for prayer for deep hurts or concerns they had in their lives. Some were hurts from a broken marriage. Others cried out for help in removing the hurt and frustrations and memories of an angry mother lashing out at them. They had no masks on! Their feelings of hopelessness were apparent, but it let me know that there were no masks in the room. God had peeled away all pride and all restrictions and they felt free to unmask their feelings and ask for help. The requests were bold as they told the group of feelings of despair over a work situation, depression, exhaustion, worry, strife, indifference, and so much emotional pain and suffering. As the masks were clearly off, it became evident who the artist of the great masks were-it was the enemy! The enemy had stamped his signature on the depression, the despair, and the destruction that filled the room.

Satan had made his presence known. The enemy wants us to feel as if we are in a deep, dark pit and we are sliding downward further and further and further. But God is standing at the top of that pit with a huge rope swinging down within reach so that we can use it to climb up out of the pit. It may take some work on our part to climb out of the pit, but God is there in His glory, in His majesty, and, yes, He knows we need Him. He wouldn't be anywhere else but right there at the top of that hole waiting for you and for me! God wants to be the first one we hug, touch, we see when we arise victorious. It is only with God's massive power that we can come out of the pit that the enemy has kicked us into time and time again. The rope is prayer. The hope is God. The hole is the Enemy. The rope of hope does exist. But just as it takes strength to climb up that rope, it will take strength to hold on tight to that rope of hope. Calling on the name of Jesus can bring strength and energy and stamina in seconds. You see, when you call on the name of Jesus, He just shows up! Every time! Every place! Everywhere! Using God's strength in our times of despair is simply the only way to become strong enough to begin climbing out of the pit of a bad relationship, the pit of sorrow, the pit of grief, the pit of an overwhelming addiction.

Reaching out to God and grabbing on to that rope of hope is as simple as praying, "God give me strength." I've been there! My conversation with God went something like this,

Lord, you know I am overwhelmed with life right now. I cannot take any more tasks, assignments, projects, problems, strife, or

indifference. I feel as if every area of my life is on the stove and the pots of water are massive. I have one pot of water that is just getting ready to boil over; it is my child. I have another pot of water that is at a full roiling boil and ready to overflow; it is work. I have two other pots of water that are at the boiling point, and I see an overflow coming. Please help me Father to see your hand and your peace in each situation. I need you!

After I finished praying for relief from each of the situations that were weighing so heavily on me, I pictured a soft, loving, gentle hand of strength and control wave across the top of each pot calming the waters to a complete stillness. I could no longer hear the pots of water even boiling. They were silenced. God's hand was upon each situation. I had gained a sure peace that only comes from the hand of God. Jesus loves all. Jesus extends His hand of love to all that call upon His name. God alone is the source for relieving burdens and bringing about calmness even when our pots are boiling out of control! Even in the midst of chaos, we cannot mask anything from God.

Taking off our masks of pride, hatred, unforgiveness, idolatry, materialism, or self-gain and coming before God humbly asking to be remade will smash that mask to bits, never to be worn again! But walking through life masking our feelings of hurt from others and pretending to be somebody we aren't will never free us to receive God's abundant blessings He has waiting for us. It would be like taking a drive through the Tennessee Valley during November or December and looking up for the glorious mountains that are situated so prominently on God's land and seeing nothing. The mountains are totally covered by a heavy fog, and they cannot even be seen. You look out and you see nothing but tremendous clouds, a blanket of heavy fog, and you just wonder what that mountain beneath the covering really looks like. Masking the mountain doesn't allow God's true beauty to arise and be seen. When the fog clears and the clouds roll away the mountains are breathtaking, adventurous, majestic, soothing, enormous, peaceful, and serene all in one glance. I believe we are God's mountains of beauty unmasked with each one claimed in Jesus name!

Chapter 24

Muscle of Love

As children of God can we really be delivered from the frustrations that consume our lives? Can we count on God to really change us? Can deliverance from our weaknesses truly be overcome or will we have to struggle the rest of our lives? Those are questions that hovered around a deeply intense conversation I had with a friend who was distraught, tired, weary, and ready just to give up on life.

As I sat listening to all of these worries and frustrations of a person whom I've known for over ten years, I saw a man of God become so worn down from battling Satan that he had become nothing more than a rag doll being pulled and torn apart every step of the way. As I listened to him describe himself, I realized that he had lost all love for himself and all respect for the man God had made. I had seen this man and his wife delivered from the bondage of sexual immorality, lust, adultery, lying, and a marriage filled with hatred, resentment, bitterness and anger. God had worked a marriage miracle in this couple's life, and the hand of Jesus delivered them from a sinful past and renewed their love for each other. So I sat prayerfully listening and asking God for direction. God was present, I moved aside and allowed the Holy Spirit to direct, redirect, and correct the thoughts that were crowding the Godly life out of this man. But moving thoughts from the enemy aside is serious business, and only the hand of a powerful God can deliver, remove and renew our minds. *Do not conform any longer to the pattern of the world, but be transformed by the renewing of your mind. Then you will be able to test and approve what God's will is – his good, pleasing and perfect will. Romans 12:2.*

"I hate the person I am. I've failed. I try, but it does no good. I'm not trying to be immoral. I'm ready just to give up. I love my wife so much, and I don't ever want to hurt her, ever! I'm just so tired of fighting it. I'm so tired.........." As I listened to those comments from a very bold, loving man of God, my heart was so saddened. It took every ounce of strength I had to sit still and hold back the tears of sorrow I had for this couple. Then I called on the Lord, and He strengthened me instantly. I sat up firmly in my chair, looked this man straight on, and the Lord began redirecting his path. God wanted him to know that, yes, he had been delivered from the sins of the past and that Satan was trying to convince him he was that old sinful man of the past. One of the enemy's best tools is using our past against us. We all have one, and you can bet it includes sin. This man was convinced that he would have to live the rest of his life in fear of his past, and that fear was crippling his future. Satan had him so fearful that he began to shut down emotionally with his wife; he had built up hatred towards himself, and he began to distance himself from God. With one small thought, Satan was robbing this man of his loving relationship with his wife, healthy emotional attitude towards himself, and worst yet, his relationship with the one and only true God. Wow! The enemy's tools are powerful! But Luke 10:19 promises us that we can overcome all the power of the enemy. All! God is more powerful than all evil spirits and demons combined!

In the midst of darkness when we think that life is not worth the effort and we cannot face any more turmoil in our lives, a God of love and mercy steps forward and puts His arms around us and tells us how to make it through our struggles. For some the struggle may be with alcohol. How do you survive in a world filled with alcohol at most every turn? For some it may be a need to control. How can you survive relinquishing control of your life in total dependence on God when you are gripped with fear of the future at every turn?

For my friend it was sexual immorality. He had fear that he might become sexually immoral again, and it would lead him down the road of destruction. God does give us aid against the enemy. It is not in our own strength that we can overcome any of these strongholds. *For with God we will gain the victory, he will trample down our enemies. Psalm 108:13.*

God has the full power to overcome all of the enemy's tactics, not just some of them but all of them! But it takes our willingness for God to invoke His power on our lives. We must be willing. If we cannot give God full power over our lives to do whatever He desires to change in us, then we cannot experience true freedom. The Lord with His infinite wisdom and sheer love for us wants us to totally and wholeheartedly give Him free reign to do whatever He needs to do with us to free us from the bondage of our past. My friend was at the point where he was desperate for relief and was willing to allow God to do anything He needed to do. That was serious stuff! He was willing to say to the Lord, I trust you so much that if you need to blind my eyes so that I cannot lust again, then just do it. As my friend and I sat in the presence of the Lord, he knew it was time. His conversation with God went something like this,

Lord, you know I can't go on like this. I cannot live this way. I'm in fear of each day of my life. I desperately want to love my wife and never, never again be in fear of lust or sexual immorality again. I give you my eyes may they never again look at anything sinful. I give you my ears may they never again hear anything immoral. I give you my hands- may they never commit immoral acts. I give you my whole body, including my mind; take it away if you need, I just can't hold anything back. You have total freedom to do whatever you need to make me whole again. I am a mighty warrior for you, and Satan has no power over me! I am going to be victorious with you Lord; you are my strength! You are my deliverance! I will not live in condemnation because of my past. My future is you, Lord God! You are my future! I will not be in bondage to the enemy's thoughts. Purify my mind. Renew my strength. Bring my wife close to me. Help us to love each other fully. Be Lord over my life. Be my strength in times of need. Be my guiding force. I will not be afraid. I will not live in Satan's lies. I am free! I am whole! I am a man of God and I will not be overcome by the enemy! In Jesus' holy name it is done! Amen and Amen and Amen!

Wow! God is so powerful. In God's loving way He showed my friend that trying in his own strength was useless and only with the power of Jesus can we overcome our enemies and our past and keep it that way. As I began praying for this man and his wife, the Lord so graciously led me to 2 Samuel 22. It is a powerful poem of praise by David after being delivered from his enemies. As I read this aloud, I knew that there would be nothing that we cannot overcome with God, nothing! God's word has all of the power we need. I pressed these verses deeply into my heart and knew that when David wrote them it was merely God himself flexing his muscle of love for His children.

David sang to the LORD the words of this song when the LORD delivered him from the hand of all his enemies and from the hand of Saul. He said: "The LORD is my rock, my fortress and my deliverer; my God is my rock, in whom I take refuge, my shield and the horn of my salvation. He is my stronghold, my refuge and my savior- from violent men you save me. I call to the LORD , who is worthy of praise, and I am saved from my enemies. 2 Samuel 22: 1-4. The LORD lives! Praise be to my Rock! Exalted be God, the Rock, my Savior! He is the God who avenges me, who puts the nations under me, who sets me free from my enemies. You exalted me above my foes; from violent men you rescued me. 2 Samuel 2:47-49.

Oh how powerful God truly is that it only takes mere breath from the Lord's nostrils for the valley of the sea to be exposed! And how much He loves us to deliver, conquer, and remove Satan's stronghold over us. We can be assured that in the midst of struggles there is one thing that is certain and one thing that can be counted on, and that is the sheer presence of God and His muscle of love.

Our Conversations with God

On Marriage

Chapter 25

Chocolate Pudding Factor

All of a sudden the chocolate pudding was at the center of our marriage, and it just happened, without any warning signs, sirens or whistles or bells going off, just chocolate pudding all over again. God with His infinite wisdom uses the simplest of things in our lives to get our attention and bring us back into His fold time and time again.

A marriage where both the husband and the wife are deeply devoted to each other and have put all mistakes aside and have chosen to follow God with all of their hearts can deeply please the heart of the Lord. But how can that relationship survive if little time is spent together nourishing and feeding each other's deepest thoughts, desires and interests? *Now then, my sons, listen to me; blessed are those who keep my ways. Listen to my instruction and be wise, do not ignore it. Proverbs 8: 32-33.* That scripture would become pressed upon our hearts as the Lord began to speak to my husband and me about nurturing our marriage. No marriage can survive without the proper nourishment. But what is nourishment for a marriage, any marriage? It took my husband and me months and months of failing desperately at nourishing our marriage before God stepped in and added some chocolate pudding.

My husband and I were pouring our hearts out to the Lord when just minutes before that, we found ourselves deep in conversation of regret, sorrow, guilt, repentance, and determination to never let our marriage go without attention again. Somehow we both failed. We were busied by our schedules, and I desperately felt neglected by David. We talked, I cried, we laughed, David hugged, I cried some more, and then we both held each other so tightly. We poured our hearts out to the Lord in a spirit of love, love for the Father and love for our marriage. David picked my head up and held my chin firmly towards his face and looked me straight in the eyes and said, "I would rather lose every single thing we have than allow our marriage to suffer." We expressed our sorrow to our heavenly Father for neglecting our marriage and asked Him to make a way for us to spend some time together. We couldn't do it on our planning because of the kids, schedules, the business, and many, many other commitments. *Again, I tell you that if two of you on earth agree about anything you ask for, it will be done for you by my Father in heaven. Matthew 18:19.* We claimed that verse over our marriage and asked God to make a way for us to have time for each other to listen, love, plan, nurture and strengthen our relationship. We had tried so desperately before to do that, but it always seemed to begin at midnight when we both were very tired and not very attentive. Our plan simply did not work no matter how hard we tried to fine-tune it.

We didn't hear anything from the Lord, but we trusted that He would provide everything we needed. Our daily lives went on and I found myself grocery shopping one warm summer day when I came across the cold section of the supermarket and stopped dead in my tracks. My legs felt heavy, my body refused to move, and the sound of my innermost thoughts began hitting me with such truth and conviction. As I gazed up at the tiny containers of chocolate pudding that my husband liked, I realized that our marriage was sitting very prominently upon the shelf awaiting attention. Those particular chocolate pudding cups I had not bought in weeks maybe even months or more. As I thought back it seemed that on each shopping trip I consciously decided not to buy them. This time it was different! A God of great concern was prominently at work in our lives, and it wasn't until I arrived home that it all became clear.

After arriving home, I proudly announced to my husband that I bought him some chocolate puddings! He said, "Wow, I haven't seen those in a long time." And then it hit me all of a sudden. It came rushing in and my spirit and I began receiving a message that was crushing. It was our marriage. Our marriage had not been given any priority in our lives in months. The move consumed us. The unpacking was so tiring, and the kids had consumed me with trying to entertain them for the summer. The non-stop company and telephone calls and e-mails poured in like a hurricane brewing in the gulf. In addition, David was very occupied with his business while I was managing a brewing storm of my own. Our marriage has been put at the very bottom of the list. We put very little time into talking together, had no time alone, offered little love and affection, and we had only the necessary communication to manage the household. Guilty, both of us, of neglecting the bond that God so delicately had woven together.

As my husband and I stopped and sat down to talk to each other, I realized that I had not been buying him the chocolate puddings because I had not felt loved lately. Not loved at all. I simply didn't want to do anything extra for him. It was sheer neglect, and feelings of resentment that brought about division. *For it is not those who hear the law who are righteous in God's sight, but it is those who obey the law who will be declared righteous. Romans 2:13.*

We knew that our marriage needed nurturing but we didn't act on that, God did! He stepped in and used some little, tiny cups of chocolate pudding to bring my husband and me to a halt in the path we were going down. We serve a God who loves us so much that He wants only the very best in our relationships with others and our relationship with Him. We could not possibly be close to the Lord with such sin in our hearts and such blatant disregard for God's call to nurture our marriage. Our conversation with God went something like this,

Dear Lord, forgive us. Forgive us for not recognizing that we've not spent our time putting our marriage in priority right under you. Cleanse us, Lord. Where we have not recognized that we had sin in our marriage, we ask that you reveal it to us now. We ask that you provide us with clarity, vision and wisdom to better plan our schedules to ensure that we love each other properly as a husband and wife should. We ask that you alone align our priorities and we submit to that alignment totally in Jesus' name. We bind the enemy from distracting us from each other, and we ask that you mold our marriage together with a bond of peace, love, and joy. Allow your spirit to cover us and awaken us should we begin to draw apart again through busyness. Quicken our thoughts to know each other's desires and allow us time to fulfill those desires. We desire you above all things, and we thank you, Father, for our marriage. May we both be pleasing to you in our words for each other, and may our marriage be rock solid, strong in Christ, and, Lord, may we always have chocolate pudding in our fridge!

Chapter 26

When God Says No

Does God tell His children no? How can we be sure it's God? Hurt, rejection and despair can make us feel so powerless and so disconnected from God, but the truth is that God is so good to us that He protects us when we don't even know we need to be protected. A "no" from God can be as loving as a mother tightly holding the hand of a young child crossing the street ensuring his safety, well being, and protection all of the way there. What have you prayed for today that you cannot see? Do you feel abandoned, lonely, depressed, or encouraged, joyful, and closer to God than ever before? *But you, dear friends, build yourself up in your most holy faith and pray in the Holy Spirit. Keep yourselves in God's love as you wait for the mercy of our Lord Jesus Christ to bring you to eternal life. Jude 1:20.*

Keeping ourselves in God's love means submitting to God's will in every single detail of our lives, even when He says "no." It's hard to understand and often difficult to see past today but God loves us so much that He provides us guidance so we can live peaceably in His will for today, and His "no" may be nothing more than His divine guidance. Well, my "no" came right in the middle of our marriage and I didn't know how to overcome it, deal with it, or even talk about it. My conversation with God went something like this,

Lord, why do I have so much trouble with this? I can't figure it out. Help me to find out why. Help me to take my rightful place up underneath the arms of my husband. It just seems every time I get there, I find a way to creep out and take the lead without even knowing it. I feel nothing good about this at all. Help me Lord.

And if there ever were a time when I didn't want to hear from God, it would have been at that moment. The Lord so boldly and gently pressed His words of truth on my heart, the conversation went something like this,

Submit. Submit. I shall provide a way for you. Continue to seek me. I shall provide a way.

And with that prayer, I knew I was getting ready to learn a lesson. The "S" word was clearly on my mind, and the Lord was getting ready to show me not only how to be "submissive" to my husband in all things, but also to allow that to become a gentle, natural yearning that would sew our marriage tightly around His loving arms. That can only, only come from God!

Submission is a formula where the leader of the home, the husband, multiplies his love over and over on his wife and that love, care, and comfort produces the natural product of submission. If there is little or no love for the wife, then the husband's formula renders a zero which when multiplied by any number, results in zero or no submission at all! *Husbands love your wives just as Christ loved the church and gave himself up for her. Ephesians 5: 25.* It takes both parts of the formula to produce submission, and if the woman refuses to submit to her husband, the product simply cannot please God. *Wives, submit to your husbands, as is fitting to the Lord. Husbands, love your wives and do not be harsh with them. Colossians 3:18-19.*

As the Lord gently held my hand and revealed His truths to me about His saying "no" and about submission, I realized several truths that I had never stopped to consider. One was about my husband, a man who was kind to me, considerate of me and very giving and loving. What a wonderful gift the Lord had given me to be able to see that clearly in my husband. But as for me, I had some work to do with my part of submission. I had a husband who was desperately trying to lead in our marriage, and I wasn't very good at following. I needed to submit first to God, then second to my husband. This happened one night in a hotel room in Chattanooga at 1:00 o'clock in the morning when God revealed His truth to me about why He said "no" and gave me my rightful place with my husband. It was a lesson of huge proportions, huge consequences and dire circumstances.

We were three weeks away from moving from Baton Rouge to Chattanooga. We had been obedient to the Lord's call to move, sell our home and relocate to Tennessee. But there was just one tiny, little problem-we didn't have anywhere to move to! This was our third trip to the city to find a house, and with each departing trip we left empty-handed. We couldn't figure it out. We knew the Lord was specific in calling us to move, but we couldn't secure a place to live. We tried on three different occasions, and on all three of those occasions none of the deals worked out. I'm sure our real estate agent was as frustrated with us as we were with ourselves. But trip number three proved very different.

We were getting nervous about selling our home and not having another one to move to, and the uncertainty was weighing heavy on our spirits. We had house shopped all day, and we were determined that with this trip we would come back with something. I scheduled houses for us to see. I talked to the real estate agent. I scouted prices. I kept an extensive folder organized with every single house on the market. I made plans. I rearranged our schedule. I made calls. I negotiated. And late that night in the hotel room after an exhausting day of house hunting, the call came. The deal on the house we tried to get fell through. Again, there was another flight, another hotel stay, and another house-hunting trip with nothing to show for it. We were so distraught that we went to the Lord in a prayer of desperation. My husband took firm hold of my hand and asked God to reveal His good and perfect will and tell us if it was meant for us to be moving at all. By the time he finished praying the whole thing became crystal clear. I could see what the entire problem was. It wasn't that God didn't want us to get a place to live. It wasn't God at all. IT WAS ME!!!! I was the problem.

As I looked up at my husband who was worn out and desperately seeking answers, God revealed to me that I was the obstacle. I was doing all of the leading, all of the leading! My husband looked, gave his opinions, and made suggestions, but that was all. He wouldn't take the lead. He would agree or disagree on a house, but he wouldn't budge from there. The enemy had placed a spirit of fear deep inside my husband that prevented him from taking his rightful place as leader and decision-maker for our family, which left us uncertain about our future. And without even knowing it, I became the leader, and God's flow of blessings stopped temporarily. My conversation with God went something like this,

Lord, I, but, if, only, but, I...........I'm sorry. Forgive me.

God proved His love and gentleness over me as His conversation with me went something like this,

Your blessings will come through your husband.

Lord, what do we do now? We need a place to live. We move in three weeks, and we have nothing.

Again, the Lord proved Himself patient once more when He spoke boldly into my mind, heart, and soul. It went something like this,

Pray that your husband will have wisdom to follow me. Pray for him to have courage and boldness and bind the enemy from producing fear and doubt. I shall never leave you nor forsake you, my child. It is my truth. I shall provide for you. Trust me. Get into your place, gently underneath your husband, and you shall be blessed.

And it was with that command that I told David everything the Lord had revealed to me. We hugged and didn't know what would happen from there. I handed the very large, expansive blue folder I was keeping on our house hunting and gave it firmly to my husband and wished him well. He took the very large folder bursting at the seams with the most frightened look I've ever seen him carry. I prayed for him to follow God's guidance and to have courage, and I felt a peace come over me that allowed me to fall gently asleep. I didn't see David again until 5:00am the next morning. He had been up all night seeking God, and he came out like a lion! He told me to get up, get dressed and he laid out five houses we were going to look at. Then he told me if we didn't like any of those, he would call and make another offer on the house I had made the offer on the day before. Wow! When the Lord gives courage and boldness, He does it big. This man was serious. He knew God's plan, and I was just along for the ride. I could feel God blessing us already. It felt so good for him to take charge. I admit it!

By 10am that morning, David had decided that he would call and make an offer on the house I had made an offer on the day before. I didn't say anything because I knew the real estate agent had told me that this particular man would not negotiate at all. I kept quiet. By 11:00am the call came in; I could only hear one side of the conversation. It was nothing more than, "....okay, good, well, okay then. We'll be in touch." I was all prepared to go back to the drawing board and start all over again house-hunting when David proudly announced that he had spoken to the real estate agent and we were all set to move in! I was shocked! That same guy yesterday wouldn't negotiate with me at all now negotiates with my husband with ease! I was speechless! But I could hear that thought playing through my mind again – let your husband lead, and I will bless you.

Whew! God clearly told me "no", and how sweet it was. *A woman should learn in quietness and full submission. 1 Timothy 2: 11. Wives, submit to your husband as to the Lord. Ephesians 5:22.* God loves us so much that He provides a way for us to survive when He says no. His way brings us so much joy and happiness, and He gently keeps us near Him. *We know that we have come to know him if we obey his commands. The man who says, "I know him," but does not do what he commands is a liar, and the truth is not in him. This is how we know we are in him: Whoever claims to live in him must walk as Jesus did. I John 2:3-6.*

God held out His massive hand of power for me to walk very easily across a balance beam that seemed too awkward to even sit on. The beam was agreeing to let David lead, no matter the seriousness of the circumstances. The Lord set me upright and took firm hold of me and steadied me so that I would 1) agree to relinquish control, 2) set my mind on someone other than myself, 3) stop making decisions for my husband, 4) accept Christ's command to fall up under my leader, 5) become selfless, 6) honor Christ, 7) respect myself and the order of leadership Christ has ordained, 8) create more love in our family unit, 9) set an example for our children, and lastly, but most importantly, 10) be obedient to God the Father.

God doesn't seek to oppress His believers, His beloved in Christ. He wants to uplift us. But what happens when God says "no" and we can't make any sense of it at all? Those are times when barren women suffer through emotional struggles with infertility or times when our loved ones are not healed from cancer or disease. We cannot make sense of God's telling us "no," but we can rest in His arms of comfort and love. We cannot possibly comprehend the mind of the Lord no matter how hard we try. *And we know that in all things God works for the good of those who love him who have been called according to his purpose. Romans 8:28.* How great is the love the Father has lavished on us, that we should be called children of God! And that is what we are!

There is always something that is yet to be given to us by the Father. It is the Father. It is the Father. It is the Father. When God says "no", He may be telling us that we need Him instead of what we are asking for. We need His comfort. We need His bold shoulders of mercy. We need His genuine hands of kindness and His ever presence in our spirit. It is the Father. A "no" from God may just mean that He will pour out on us His love that immerses us in a thick flow of His strength, courage and determination that allows us to feel the very presence of Him. This would not have been possible if the answer had been yes. It is the Father.

God, the Father

Tremendous steps, holy glory, eyes of gold.
That is the Father our God of old.

Commanding light, redeeming ones
in his sight, that is the Father.

Maker of creation, humanity and yes even you and me,
that is the work of the Father.

Ask it in my son's name the Father proclaims.
It is his will that dominates our own,
It is the Father.

Strong, overwhelming in his glory
an everlasting presence over all,
It is the Father.

Who has your life so tightly wound in
throughout the Son, it is the Father.

Ever present, all full of creation
and his wrath my come upon the land with just
one stoke of his hand.

It is the Father.
It is the Father.
It is the Father.

So loving to his people and so totally present to all.
*That is **our** Father, God to the very small.*

God does tell His children "no" time and time again. But until we can look into the Father's heart and see that His "no" is His immersing power of love on us, it is only then can we truly gain comfort, assurance, peace, and tranquility. That is the Father!

Chapter 27

Sex, Marriage and God?

C an sex be a God thing? Can you talk to God about sex? Can
sex be used to emanate a Christ like relationship between a
husband and a wife? If you answered yes to all of the above questions, skip forward to the next chapter. If you're not so sure about
those questions, then let's talk sex, marriage, and God.

God has clear principles that He has set forth in His word about
marriage and sex. *Marriage should be honored by all, and the
marriage bed kept pure, for God will judge the adulterer and all the
sexually immoral. Hebrews 13:4.* Do we have enough strength of
our own to keep our marriage pure, clean, and free from all sexual
sin? I believe apart from Him we can do nothing!

Marriage is an equation where one plus one equals one. *For this
reason a man will leave his father and mother and be united to his
wife, and they will become one flesh. Genesis 2:24.* We are joined to
our spouses emotionally, spiritually, and intellectually by a bond of
commitment, love, honor, desire and yearning that often challenges
human reasoning. Desire is powerful and consuming and is no
surprise to God. God intended that yearning to be a part of our
marriage relationship. *Your desire will be for your husband, and he
will rule over you. Genesis 3:15b.* Desire for our spouse is part of
that emotional and spiritual attachment we have in marriage. Desire
done God's way can lead to a more powerful marriage relationship,

a stronger bond of commitment and an unexplainable yearning to be closer and closer to our spouse.

What happens when our desires go outside of our marriage? Simple. Desires can be deadly not done God's way! God's desires for our marriage relationship haven't changed. He hasn't changed the rules or even bent them one little bit since he gave the Ten Commandments to Moses. *Jesus Christ is the same yesterday and today and forever. Hebrews 13:8.* God's supreme wisdom gives us the formula for keeping our marriage healthy, whole and blessed. We bring in things into our marriage relationship that simply don't include God's plan for our lives. The marriage relationship is between a husband and a wife period. That relationship does not include other women or men. Now we might not actually walk a person in our home and say, "Honey, I'd like you to meet Johnny. He's going to be another component in our marriage for a little while, okay dear?" But Satan is very clever, and he wants to bring about division, havoc, and chaos in our marriage relationship.

Temptations will come. We are not guaranteed a marriage free of temptation. But our Lord, who knows us deeply provided a way to overcome temptations. It is available by simply asking God to provide you with a pure marriage relationship and the ability to do His will day in and day out. *No temptation has seized you except what is common to man. And God is faithful; he will not let you be tempted beyond what you can bear. But when you are tempted, he will also provide a way out so that you can stand up under it. I Corinthians 10: 13.* Marriage done God's way will never, never bring another partner into the marriage whether it be one time or a billion times, whether in sex or attraction or just an attachment. Never ever believe that what a man and his wife do in their bedroom is their own business! That is a lie from the devil's hell! If you use pornography in your sexual relationship with your spouse to spark desire or if you think about sex in any immoral way, it departs from God's plan for you and your spouse. Bringing in any other partner into your sexual relationship with your spouse whether in mind, thought, or action simply cannot and does not please our heavenly Father. God's plan for His people is to bless us beyond what we even can imagine, but the flow of blessings can stop if we don't abide in God's word with our marriage. *A man of perverse heart does not prosper; he whose tongue is deceitful falls into trouble. Proverbs 17:20. He who conceals his sins does not prosper, but whoever confesses and renounces them finds mercy. Proverbs 28:13.* My husband and I had a very intimate conversation with God on our sex life and it went something like this,

Lord, we need you. We love each other and so desperately want to please you from each kiss to each passionate lovemaking session. Show us, guide us, and free us from any and all sin that is sexual in nature, and bring to us your plan for our sex lives. We seek you. We ask you. We want your plan, not ours. Show us. Guide us. You are our master alone. How we need you!

And that prayer, sparked a whole avenue of thoughts; topics, and ultimately the formula that God laid deeply on our hearts for our marriage and our sex life. That formula can be traced all of the way back to the Ten Commandments. God's commandments tell us how to please Him in our relationship with others and our relationship with Him. Do you put God first in your marriage, or is your mate at the top, or worse yet, are *you* at the very top? Do you worship your mate or your marriage? Before you automatically answer that one, let's look deep into a marriage that I know well – mine. God revealed Himself to me in His commanding power one day that affected our marriage so powerfully that I can still feel the hands of change on our marriage that God so lovingly wove into our lives so long ago.

My husband is a helper by nature. Any problem or circumstance that I have found myself in since I have been married to David has always seemed to be solved, satisfied, or avoided by my simply calling out to David for help. If my job wasn't going so well, I called David. If I was having problems with the children, I called David. If I couldn't make it through my day, I called David. I had him programmed on speed dial for any and every emergency that crept up. I didn't have God on speed dial! I depended on David for problem solving, emotional support and basically anything life held for me- until God stepped in and revealed to me that David was merely a man and not God.

The Lord spoke to my spirit so deeply during the course of one problem that I faced, and revealed to me that David could not solve, help or cure this problem, and only God could help me, encourage me, and ultimately deliver me. God allowed me to face dire circumstances to turn my attention from David to God completely. It was simply one of the most difficult things I've ever encountered. God in His infinite mercy forgave me for putting David first and so delicately revealed it to me and then provided me with care that was immeasurable. My husband's love for me and the gentleness he used in solving my problems could not compare to the hands of our Lord and Master who is all- knowing, all-giving and desires us to come to Him and be fully dependent on Him. I learned from that painful period in my life and placed David in his rightful place right beneath God, since then our marriage has grown, developed, and been nurtured by the very hands of God.

God got right in the middle of our marriage and shoved out all of the things not of Him and put up a sign for a period of time that said, "Warning, under construction!" He changed, rewired, and halted all of the enemy's work. What a sweet time of love, nurturing and romance we began experiencing. God simply wants to be at the center of our marriage, and in every detail, including our sex life!

That's right; God even wants to be at the center of our sex life. He is intimately woven into our marriage, and our marriage includes sex, so you guessed it, God is interested in our sex life! God knows every sexual thought you have ever had! God tells us what is good sexually and what is not good. *Put to death, therefore whatever belongs to your earthly nature: sexual immorality, impurity, lust, evil desires and greed, which is idolatry. Colossians 3:5. But among you there must not be even a hint of sexual immorality, or any kind of impurity or of greed, because these are improper for God's holy people. Ephesians 5:3.*

Sex in marriage is an act of romantic love and intimacy between a husband and a wife that fulfills human desires, releases our love and allows us to delight in each other. That type of romantic love can be as a simple as praise and adoration for our spouse or as loving and gentle as his or her touch. *Like an apple tree among the trees of the forest is my lover among the young men. I delight to sit in his shade, and his fruit is sweet to my taste. He has taken me to the banquet hall, and his banner over me is love. Song of Songs 2: 3-4.*

When our children are small, we go to great efforts to praise even the most basic of things, like using the potty or identifying the alphabet correctly. As they grow, we begin to praise their choice of friends or their grades. We spend a lifetime praising our children, but why? Could it be we are nurturing our relationship with them and helping them to grow perhaps? Marriage and sex in marriage are very similar to that. We take great pleasure when our spouses compliment our hair or our clothes or the ultimate, our bodies! When the compliments truly come from the heart, they pour into us the power to connect with that person in a unity and love that begin to nurture that relationship and grow it into permanence. Sex between a husband and a wife can be powerful, connecting, refreshing, rejuvenating, loving and nurturing or it can be dreadful, painful, saddening, or just routine.

God knows your hurts, your desires and your needs for your sex life. If you find yourself dead tired day after day just from keeping up with the pace of the world and not desiring sex with your spouse, then ask God to reveal to you how you can overcome it. Be sincere. He knows your thoughts before you speak them. He has the power to bring us more energy and more stamina into our lives. And if the problem is deeply rooted into your entire being, then know that we serve a Risen Savior who is the ultimate healer and deliverer of all hurts, traumas, and misery. Jesus alone can take away, remove, cleanse and refresh your mind, your thoughts and your body. Go to the Father in prayer and ask Him to reveal your pain, remove your pain, and diminish any hurt you have suffered sexually, and you will walk away refreshed and ready to enjoy your sex life with your spouse. You will develop a more satisfying sexual relationship that is free of pain and above all, pleasing to our heavenly Father. And if your sex life is dull, drab, and routine and gives you little satisfaction, the answer may be more open communication with your spouse about your feelings. Odd as it seems, I had a friend who remained deeply troubled by many facets of her relationship with her husband, and if you asked her husband, he was totally clueless as to any problem existing at all. They simply hadn't talked about the problems, so her husband just wasn't aware of them. Seek the Lord in prayer before you communicate your feelings to your spouse about your sex life. Remember, the enemy stands ready to attack your relationship. *Be self-controlled and alert. Your enemy the devil prowls around like a roaring lion looking for someone to devour. Resist him, standing firm in the faith, because you know that your brothers throughout the world are undergoing the same kind of suffering. I Peter 5: 8-9.* Beginning a conversation about your dissatisfaction with sex can come out in the form of angry or bitter words that only hurt the relationship more or it can be gentle and Spirit-led, free of strife and result in change that can glorify God. Pray for wisdom and guidance before you utter the very first word to your spouse! You'll be glad you did!

There are so many more blessings when you include God in your marriage and your sex life. You enjoy obedience, gratification, and heavenly rewards and, yes, even the icing on the cake. There is no sweeter place than to take firm hold of your spouse's hand after making love and praying to our heavenly Father. My husband and I have experienced the supernatural time and time again after making love and then pressing our bodies closely together and praying to our Lord and King. I remember the first time David grabbed my hand to pray after we made love, our bodies unclothed and naked, our love so intimate and yes, he grabbed my hand and said, "Let's thank God." He so intimately spoke to the Father about his love for me and his desires being fulfilled and gave praise to our Lord and King so preciously that it drew us together and nearer to the Father all in the same breath. It was truly a supernatural experience. Don't miss out on an opportunity to get that closeness with your spouse and ultimately with our Heavenly Father by skipping that part of sex. I remember so vividly as I leaned in as close as I could get to David that day, our naked bodies comfortable and my head nestled on his shoulder, I felt a peace that was consuming, loving and so fulfilling. We drew closer to each other by drawing closer to our Heavenly Father in prayer. From that moment on, there have been so many times when we have gone to the Father in prayer after loving each other so intimately. For David and me, that truly is the icing on the cake!!!

Our Conversations with God

On Resting in Him

Chapter 28

Job for a Day

What do you think of when you hear the Old Testament name Job? What would you say to Job if you were face-to-face with this man who was about to face tragic losses in just a matter of minutes? Would you agree to be Job for a day, a week, a month or longer if asked? I believe that each of us tries in our deepest of hearts to avoid tragedy, sadness and sorrow, so why does God allow those things to come upon us? I believe in God's infinite wisdom He so lovingly desires us to obtain the faithfulness of Job and all that He has for us that He allows circumstances in our lives that we see as tragic, devastating, depleting, and without reason. It is that sense of total dependence on God that brings us into His throne room and ultimately brings sweet relief when turbulent times hit. My turbulent time was upon me.

I awoke one morning to find God waiting for me in a very unusual place that I had not seen or felt before. It took a bit for me to get there but in God's loving arms of patience, He waited for me to come to Him and receive His limitless love. God took me by the hand that day and opened my eyes to see His sovereignty, His overwhelming compassion for His children, and His perfect, perfect love for you and for me all through a man named Job. *So Satan went out from the presence of the Lord and afflicted Job with painful sores from the soles of his feet to the top of his head. Then*

Job took a piece of broken pottery and scraped himself with it as he sat among the ashes. His wife said to him, "Are you still holding on to your integrity? Curse God and die!" He replied, "You are talking like a foolish woman. Shall we accept good from God, and not trouble? In all this, Job did not sin in what he said. Job 2:7-10. We cannot imagine all that Job lost. It is enormous and gut wrenching to think of Job's losses; it is difficult to comprehend a man losing his sons and daughters, his means of survival, his friends, and his health just like that. As I sat and pondered Job and his turmoil, I began to see a slight resemblance to what I was experiencing in my own life at the time.

At one particular moment in time, God allowed my health to be uncertain, my relationships to be far from me, my finances to be rocky, my husband and family to be distant, and my church family to be removed just like that! It was problem mounted on top of problem and turmoil facing turmoil. As I sat emotionally battered and beaten, my conversation with God went something like this,

Lord, I see what you have wanted me to see now. It is you. I have nothing at all at this moment except you. It is you that you want me to see. I am here. Take me.

And it was with that prayer that the Lord spoke deep into my heart and shared His perfect love for me. He took away the things that I held dear and close to my heart and allowed me to be totally stripped and come before his throne with nothing on my heart, my mind, or "need list" except Him. It was the one time in my life that I can honestly say that I didn't need for anything except the love of the Father. It was with that love that I gained freedom from the turmoil around me.

God allowed me to experience turmoil in overwhelming areas of my life in huge proportions in order to show me that Jesus is all I really need. All of those other things in my life are simply bonuses. Sweet bonuses! Jesus is the gem, and the other things such as good health, a loving family, sound finances, and nurturing relationships are God's love being poured out over us by His warm, soothing hand of kindness. *It is better to take refuge in the Lord than to trust in man. Psalm 118:8.* Taking refuge in the Lord is the only place of peace that I have found to be true in the midst of turmoil. Simply getting before the Father with nothing except ourselves- not our children or our jobs or our spouses takes us deeper into the Father's love inch by inch. As I crept into the hands of the Lord, all fear passed away, and I remained calm in the midst of crisis, turmoil, division, and uncertainty.

Picture God waiting on your doorstep. The inside of your home is at unrest. You may have children that have fallen away from God, or you may have a marriage that is unsettled or you may have financial problems that seem beyond recovery or a job that seems hopeless or you may be facing a life of singleness; whatever the magnitude of the problem, God is waiting on your doorstep. He desires you to remove yourself from your situation and come sit with Him. God is present in times of trouble, but God is not pain and suffering, He is the relief from the pain and suffering. God is waiting on the outside where it is peaceful, calm, and soothing. He may not be waiting out there with $10,000 to pay off your credit cards, and He may not be waiting out there with a pill that will heal your spouse's cancer, but He is sovereign. His love is so overwhelming in the midst of sorrow, pain, and suffering.

As you picture God sitting on your doorstep, imagine peeking outside to get a glimpse of what peace and joy really look like during the midst of struggles but you can't see anything. You are not in the presence of the Lord. You are still removed from Him. You have to open the door, step out, and shut off the world behind you and sit side-by-side with your Lord and Savior. You have to leave the things that are troubling you behind and focus on God alone. As you sit on the doorstep with your arms folded around your knees, you begin to feel a warming on your back that inches up your spine all of the way to your fingers and back down to the bottom of your feet. Your body becomes stilled and focused. You are in the presence of the Lord. There is no more worry, anxiety, and turmoil, fear of the future, or any uncertainty. It has been removed. You lean over towards your Lord and Savior, and He places His massive arm of protection over your shoulder. You lean in closer. As your shoulder touches His shoulder, your insurmountable problems pass from you to Him. You sit together in silence. Words are not needed. You have gained peace beyond belief and an overwhelming joy that just minutes before seemed impossible. Imagine Jesus on your doorstep holding you and shouldering your burdens. *"Come to me, all you who are weary and burdened, and I will give you rest. Matthew 11:28.*

Bearing a slight resemblance to Job for a day wasn't what I expected when I got up that morning, but God desired me to be with Him as never before. He knows best. I do not. It is so hopeful that during the midst of testing, struggles, and trials we have a God who deeply cares for us and who can give us rest! It is faith at its fullest and peace in its privacy and joy in Jesus that bring us our finest moments, our hour of need, and the loving hand of God for the whole world to see.

Chapter 29

Mounting Differences

*B*efore *I formed you in the womb I knew you, before you were born I set you apart; I appointed you as a prophet to the nations. Jeremiah 1:5.* Being set apart is not necessarily one of those things we long for on a daily basis. I don't imagine Jeremiah awoke one morning and said, "Lord, just set me apart; I want to be different!" But the truth is God set Jeremiah apart divinely, before he was formed! Before that baby boy took his first breath, God had already planned his life and, yes, set him apart! Jeremiah's situation is more common to us than we realize. We go about and plan our lives, our careers, our futures just as Jeremiah did, and then God halts man's plans abruptly, swiftly, and in His infinite wisdom. We might be whistling merrily along when God walks up and says, "HEY, HEY! YES, YOU! I've got something for you. Come see." I envision myself turning around and looking behind me to see whom God is really talking to when I realize that there is no one behind me. It's me! It's you! God doesn't just want part of us, our lives; He wants all of us fully! God longs for His children, His workers, His manpower to awaken and beckon for His hand of mounting differences to form over us and cover us fully and completely so we can go about the Father's business.

Going about the Father's business comes with unique challenges and multitudes of blessings, blessings of gaining strength through the Father, peace through the Son and joy through the Spirit despite the opposition planted firmly around us. Our Lord has given us the ability to turn our differences that the world may see as odd into great works of faith and tremendous steps of boldness for the cause of Christ. Boldness does not necessarily mean standing on the street corner preaching to the whole world, it may mean for you or for me to boldly seek God to find out just where He would like us to serve in His ministry. Now that's boldness because you never, never know what the answer might be should you dare ask the Lord for guidance! It means you are courageous enough to overstep your bounds. It means that you are so deeply confident, not in yourself but in God. God can bring those into the fold; He can split hearts wide open for His love; He can nudge His servants along to a higher level of service. It's not us! It is God's power being poured into us like a massive fuel tank pushing and propelling us forward each day to accomplish the Father's business. So when God calls us to be bold for Christ and we don't find ourselves particularly apt in that area, we can rest in God. *In the same way, the Spirit helps us in our weaknesses. Romans 8:26a.* My husband and I have seen up close and personal how God can take that verse and thrust His might, His power, and His strength on us to make us strong where we are truly lacking endurance, strength, and courage. For my husband, that lesson came in the form of work, mounting differences, and very trying circumstances.

For David providing for his family was a very big deal, so when the Lord called my husband to quit his job and didn't give any direction for future employment, he had to trust with every ounce of strength he had. So for David, quitting his job and not opening his business until almost a year later was his future! I don't know about you, but how many men do you know who would quit their jobs and wait on the Lord to provide for all of their needs indefinitely with no visible sign of employment in the future? For my husband it could not be done in man's strength; it truly took the strength of the Lord to be able to wait indefinitely for a plan, a method of employment, and a means of survival. He found himself in a very unusual situation; yes, he realized that his situation was quite odd as the Lord had uniquely put him in that situation, and his only job was to trust the Lord's plan with all of his heart.

When God reaches out and gives us a unique situation that sets us apart from the world, it's simply His hand of love transforming our lives so we can live more like the Son each day. *For I am not seeking my own good but the good of many, so that they may be saved. Follow my example, as I follow the example of Christ. 1 Corinthians 10: 33b.* Certainly David's job situation was unique, but God used those differences to challenge us spiritually, awaken our faithfulness to Him, and ultimately bring about a multitude of unexpected blessings. With those differences firmly on our mind, we went to the Lord in prayer for full and complete surrender to those differences as He willed. Our conversation with God went something like this,

Lord, thank you for the differences you have placed in our family. Unique as those differences are, we see they are you. You have humbled our spirits, and we acknowledge any ways that are not pleasing to you. Specifically, if we have any desire to remove those differences, we ask for cleansing and forgiveness, dear God. We want to submit every area of our lives to you and we ask that our differences only glorify you and not ourselves. Lord, where we have not been different and have walked in the way of the world, we ask for forgiveness. Remove any spirit of unrighteousness and allow us to praise you always for making us unique. We want to use our God-given abilities and talents to help encourage others in this world and to bring you praise, honor, and glory. Remove any hindrance that prevents us from using the things you have given us in accordance to your will. Where we have not used our talents to your glory, reveal them to us. Give us an accepting spirit and help us to change. Strengthen us this day to continue to walk in appreciation for our differences in Jesus' name. Amen and Amen.

Resting in God in our moments of differences brings such bewildering moments to a shocking close. It is that rest and nurturing that allow our mounting differences to surface on the outside while awakening our inside!

Chapter 30

Pit Stop

Stopping and taking time out to rest, relax, and rejuvenate our bodies may be the last thing on our minds when our lives are the very busiest. Jesus himself walked this earth and had so many begging for His time, His attention, His healing, and all that He found it necessary to escape into the Father's hand for rest. But how can we come into the Lord's presence when our schedules, our lives, our children's lives, and so many other obligations are present? Simple. By asking God to intervene in our lives in any way He sees fit to accomplish His will. I found myself there early one Saturday morning as I struggled just to just get out of bed.

For weeks my body had been screaming for rest, and I ignored its call for solitude and rest. I kept on going and kept on scheduling, doing, and planning while ignoring every call my body made to me for recharging. Slipping away from God spiritually was as easy as marking in another "to-do" on the calendar. God is so loving and so merciful that even when we don't pray over our schedules or talk to God about the things that are keeping us busy in our lives, He is still there waiting for us to turn to Him. And on that Saturday morning when my body refused to cooperate and get out of bed, my conversation with God went something like this,

Lord, Lord, please give me strength.

As I quietly rested in bed, I felt the Lord speaking deeply into my heart and I knew the only place I would get rest was in God's word. *"It is written, Man does not live on bread alone, but on every word that comes from the mouth of God." Matthew 4:4.* God's word is God Himself. Our seeking to know God and understand His word is as lovely to God as a soft gentle kiss to His very face. I found myself embracing God and loving Him through His word, and somehow I knew that His word was really where I needed to be and the other things of the day were not so important after all. I found myself deep in thought over God's word. I called out to the Lord for insight and understanding. He answered. I am convinced that getting into the presence of God through prayer or the reading of God's word each day cannot be substituted, underestimated, or taken out as it is as necessary as breathing!

Rest in God

Rest in God and this day is done.
Rest in God and you shall never yearn for the Holy one.

Rest in Jesus and all your cares
shall never see a new day's light.
Rest in Him and let Jesus be your sight.

Rest in Him and your mind will quicken.
Rest in Him and the day's tasks shall lessen.

Rest in Him and take hold of His Word.
Rest in Him and know that the Savior is true.
Rest in Him before all that you do!

Being in the presence of the Lord is the ultimate and the highest reward we can seek. Missing out on being with the Holiest of holies, the King of kings, the Lord God Almighty was my "Martha Moment". *But Martha was distracted by all of the preparations that had to be made. She came to him and asked, "Lord, don't you care that my sister has left me to do the work by myself? Tell her to help me!" "Martha, Martha, the Lord answered, you are worried and upset about many things, but only one thing is needed. Mary has chosen what is better, and it will not be taken away from her." Luke 10: 40-41.*

Martha moments are our opportunities to reach beyond the busyness of our lives and put all things aside for the one thing that is really significant, highly honorable, and truly needed- our time with God. Wasting time, burning minutes, and eliminating the seconds on the clock are the enemy's way of keeping us so busy that we cut off our life support- our time with God.

We may have very good intentions, but when we busy ourselves, we stand to lose so much more from that busyness than if we would had done what Jesus would have chosen to do in that same situation. I can remember so many times having company over, and I can see them sitting at the bar in the kitchen while I was standing over the sink busily putting dishes away or clanging pots and pans after dinner instead of just enjoying their company. Oh, how much I must have missed by not focusing solely on my company and focusing instead of the condition of the kitchen. My sweet, sweet sister-in-law, Gerri Lowe, knows the benefit and the art of focusing on her company. I can remember so many times when we visited her that she always kept her preparations to a minimum and her conversations to a maximum. She prepared for her company modestly but adequately; oftentimes we ate sandwiches for lunch, but we had wonderful, loving talks after lunch with her sitting at the table focused on nothing but us. And other times when the dinner may have been more extravagant Gerri still didn't deviate from focusing on those around her, loving us in God's way and making sure that the busyness of the kitchen did not outweigh her time spent with her company. Having a home that is warm, inviting, and filled with hospitality is a God thing. But unless we consciously take those pit stops when our guests arrive the busyness overtakes us, and we follow Martha's path again and again and again.

Pit stops may mean peaceful moments of solitude used to rest in the arms of the Savior, or it may mean focusing on those around us in the quietness of our homes. Either way, Jesus is present. Taking pit stops can produce a greater measure of love for those around us and produce a more energized body, a spirit more in tune to God's will, and a mind that is sharpened to God's ways. Massive works by the Savior in huge proportions and quantities unlimited are available for you and for me by simply resting, resting in God.

Yes, God does call His children to rest, rest in Him. As children of God we cannot gain the eyes of Christ, the heart of the Lord, and the feet of Jesus if we don't seek Him in extreme. Taking your pit stop won't slow you down, it will raise you up; it will quicken your step and make you a tower of strength, a pillar of love, and bring Glory to His name! *The name of the Lord is a strong tower, the righteous run to it and are safe. Proverbs 18: 10.* Nestle up to God today and bathe your body in the luxury of God's presence and the company of your Lord and Savior!

But when he, the Spirit of truth, comes,
he will guide you in to all truth. He will not speak on his own;
he will speak only what he hears,
and he will tell you what is yet to come.
John 16:13

You have made known to me the path of life; you will fill me with
joy in your presence, with eternal pleasures at your right hand.
Psalm 16:11

As the scripture says, "Anyone who trust in him
will never be put to shame."
Romans 10:11

Bibliography

Morehead, A., & Morehead L., (1981). The New American Webster Handy College Dictionary. New York: Penguin Books USA.

Syswerda, Jean E. (2001). Women of Faith Study Bible New International Version. Michigan: Zondervan Publishing House.

Printed in the United States
18059LVS00003B/76-255